Quick Guide to America Online 5.0

Jennifer Watson
and Dave Marx

Quick Guide to America Online 5.0

Published by
America Online, Inc.
22000 AOL Way
Dulles, VA 20166
www.aol.com (America Online Web site)

Library of Congress Control Number: 00-104747

ISBN: 0-7645-3528-5

1O/QV/QW/QQ/IN

Printed in the United States by America Online, Inc.

Credits

America Online

Cover Design:
DKG Design, Inc

IDG Books Worldwide

Acquisitions and Editorial

Editors:
Kim Darosett,
Tonya Maddox

Acquisitions Editor:
Kathy Yankton

Editorial Manager:
Leah Cameron

Publishing Director:
Andy Cummings

Production

Project Coordinator:
Melissa Ward

Layout and Graphics:
Kathie Schutte; Brian Torwelle

Proofreader:
Brian Massey

Indexer:
Sharon Hilgenberg

Navigating Through This Book

Check out the Table of Contents or each chapter's introductory bullets for an overview of chapter contents. Try the Index if you're looking for something specific. And please see the following sections for information on helpful conventions that we use throughout the book.

Key Combinations and Menu Selections

AOL offers plenty of keyboard shortcuts for quicker, easier use. When possible, we give relevant key combinations for various features in the text. For example, Ctrl+M is the keyboard shortcut to open a new Write Mail window. Ctrl refers to the key labeled *Ctrl* on your Windows keyboard, and the + symbol tells you to hold down the Ctrl key while typing the following letter — in this case, *M*.

Icons

We call your attention to important concepts and information throughout the book by using the following icons:

Tips provide you with extra knowledge that separates the novice from the pro.

Notes provide additional or critical information and technical data on the current topic.

Definitions explain terms and concepts.

Cross references show you places where you can find more information on a particular topic.

Find It Online icons direct you to a location on AOL or the Internet.

Table of Contents

Chapter 1

Introducing AOL

In This Chapter

- Discover what you can see and do on America Online
- Learn how you can communicate with family and friends
- Create a distinctive new screen name and secure password
- Find help in all the right places
- Look over the unique features and services of America Online

Welcome, everyone! Your guides for a quick tour around America Online are Jennifer Watson and Dave Marx, authors of *Your Official America Online Tour Guide,* from which this Quick Guide is adapted. Now, settle back and enjoy the view as we give you a glimpse into the wonders of America Online.

AOL and the Internet

America Online means many things to many people. By itself, AOL is a community of over 22 million members — individuals, families, and companies. You can meet and interact with groups of your fellow AOL members in chat rooms; on public message boards; in live, one-on-one Instant Messages; and, of course, through e-mail. AOL's community is so large and its offerings so diverse that you might never be tempted to stray beyond its comforting borders. That would be a shame, though.

America Online is also part of a much wider world, the international computer network known as the *Internet*. All the wonders and riches of the Internet are available to AOL's members at no additional charge. You can exchange e-mail and view World Wide Web sites anywhere on the globe. So, AOL and the Internet make up a global community where nearly any need for information and interaction can be quickly satisfied.

What Is AOL?

In a technical sense, America Online is a proprietary online service, which uses its own customized systems. You must use AOL software to make use of the AOL service. This allows AOL to tightly integrate its many features so that you can chat, exchange e-mail, surf the World Wide Web, download files, check your stock portfolio, and much more — all at the same time, with great ease and safety.

AOL operates the world's largest Internet-access network. You can access AOL from over 140 countries around the world, and after you connect to AOL, you're also connected to the entire Internet. Even when you don't have access to a computer running AOL software, you can still access your AOL e-mail and AOL buddies via any computer connected to the World Wide Web, thanks to AOL Mail (on the Web) and AOL Instant Messenger.

Communicate with People through E-mail and Elsewhere

Community is an important word around AOL. It means that online areas not only deliver information and services, but also create places where people can meet, connect, and share their knowledge and interests. First, there's e-mail, the silent giant of AOL. People exchange more than 67 million e-mail messages over AOL every day!

Millions of members join AOL just so they can hear that famous voice say, "You've got mail!" You can address one message to dozens of people and instantly share news, views, and even photos with families, friends, and business associates all over the world. What's more, you may start hearing back from them within minutes. See Chapter 3 for more information on e-mail.

Using e-mail is just the start. AOL offers you other ways — outlined in the following list and expanded on in Chapter 4 — to broaden your online communications and strengthen the ties to your family and friends:

- **Instant Messages** (private, one-on-one live chats) and **Buddy Lists** (which tell you what friends are online) work together to give you a sense of always being connected to your friends and loved ones.

- **Chat rooms** provide a great way to meet people from all over the world.
- **Message boards** on topics of every description give people a chance to share their questions, answers, and thoughts with people of like interest.
- **Conferences** are live events that bring thousands of people together for interviews with movers, shakers, and stars.

Keep Up-to-Date

From the moment you sign on to the moment you sign off, there's a world of news and information swirling around you. Monitor the news ticker at AOL News, keep abreast of the financial markets, and keep your eyes on the sports scoreboard, all at the same time. And the current weather report is just a click away. Chapter 6 gives you information on how to customize news service through AOL News Profiles.

AOL's newest feature, My Calendar, is an electronic appointment book custom-tailored to your needs and interests. My Calendar's Event Directory has lists of online events, concerts, TV shows, and sporting events. Click the items you want to appear on your calendar, and they are added automatically. You can also schedule one-time or recurring events for yourself, your friends, and family — then share those events with anyone else who has My Calendar. More details about My Calendar are in Chapter 5.

Manage Your Finances and Spend Money

Everyone has a nest egg to build and bills to pay, and those jobs get more complicated with each passing day. With AOL's Personal Finance Channel, you can trade stocks, manage your bank accounts, pay bills, shop for a home, apply for a mortgage, obtain insurance quotes, and get help with financial aid for your college-age children, all without leaving the comfort of your home!

In addition to managing your money, AOL can help you spend it a bit more wisely. AOL is the biggest shopping destination on the Internet. Shop for everything for your home, from kitchen appliances to a computer Zip drive. For that matter, let AOL help you shop for your next home, too! And through your AOL connection, you can get airline tickets, theater tickets, movie tickets, and concert tickets, and, if you do your banking online, you can even pay for parking tickets. See Chapter 8 for more details on shopping online.

Note: AOL and its retailing partners go to great lengths to create a safe online shopping environment. Your credit card information is carefully protected, AOL's Certified Merchants Program promises the highest standards of customer service and quality, and AOL stands directly behind those merchants with its own money-back guarantee.

Learn New Things and Explore Old Interests

AOL is full of information on a vast array of topics, from the most personal to the most professional. Whether you're looking for specific information or just want to browse around on your own, AOL has something for you. To learn more about exploring your interests on AOL, see Chapter 7.

Your search can start right at the top with AOL's Welcome screen (see Figure 1-1), where you find all of AOL's information organized into 18 channels, each one focused on an area of interest to AOL members. We give you an overview of these channels in Chapter 9.

Contribute Something

Thanks to AOL's connection to the fabled information superhighway, you can contribute your spirit and knowledge to the whole world, or just reach family and friends who have access to America Online and/or the Internet. Exchange files and pictures in libraries, voice your opinions and experiences on message boards, organize a chat in the People Connection, and even publish to the World Wide Web — AOL provides the means. Every screen name of an AOL member account can create a home page on the Web at no extra cost. And when you have a Web page, you've become a citizen of the world.

Click a button in this column to visit one of 18 channels.

Figure 1-1. The AOL Welcome screen offers 18 channels to broaden your interests and harbor your hobbies.

Signing Up and Signing On

Before you embark on your AOL adventures, you need a few travel essentials. Namely, you need a computer capable of running the AOL software, a copy of the AOL software itself, a way to pay for the AOL service, and some ideas for screen names.

The Computer

AOL software version 5.0 for Windows requires a Pentium-class PC. Your computer should have at least 16 megabytes of RAM, 30 megabytes of available hard disk space, a monitor capable of displaying at least 256 colors at 640 x 480 resolution, and a 14,400 Kbps or faster modem. Also required is Windows 95 or Windows 98.

AOL software version 5.0 for the Mac requires a Power Macintosh with at least 32 megabytes of RAM. Your Mac should also have 30 megabytes of available hard disk space, a monitor capable of displaying 356 colors at 640 x 800 resolution (though 800 x 600 is preferable), and a 14,400 Kbps or faster modem. Also required is version 8.1 or higher of the Mac operating system.

The Software

The latest version of AOL software is version 5.0, which is usually distributed on CD-ROM. If you're unable to find an AOL CD-ROM, you have several options:

- You can call AOL at 1-800-827-6364 and request a sign-on kit. (We recommend this option.)
- If you already have Internet access, point your Web browser to `www.aol.com`, and download the software from AOL's Web site.
- If you have AOL service, you can visit Keyword: **Upgrade** on AOL itself.

To install the software and sign up with AOL, insert the CD-ROM disc or execute the installer program you downloaded. On-screen directions guide you through the installation and setup process. If you have problems during installation or setup, feel free to call AOL at 800-346-3704 (Windows) or 800-265-8007 (Mac).

The Screen Name(s)

AOL (and the rest of the world) needs to know how to address you when you're online. You can select up to seven identities for yourself and/or other members of your family.

Definition The online identities that you set up are called *screen names*, and they may come to mean nearly as much to you and your friends as your real name or your street address. Come to think of it, on America Online screen names are your real name and street address.

A screen name travels with you (and identifies you) wherever you go on AOL, whether you're in a chat room, posting to a message board, or writing e-mail. Your screen name is also your e-mail address. If you write e-mail to `JenniferAndDave` from your AOL account, it comes straight to us. If a friend on the Internet sends us e-mail, it is addressed to `JenniferAndDave@aol.com`.

Why the difference? The `@aol.com` (pronounced "At A O L dot com") part of the second address is like the city, state, and country on a regular postal address. Folks out on the Internet have to specify that our e-mail be sent to AOL instead of some other online service. AOL knows that e-mail lacking the `@` symbol gets delivered locally.

Consider setting up a separate screen name for each family member. Doing so has these advantages:

- Each screen name has its own rights and privileges, including a Buddy List, Personal Filing Cabinet, Online Mailbox, member profile, and other customizable features.
- Any message or chat line you send automatically carries your screen name.
- You save the expense of additional AOL accounts for various members of your family.
- Parental Controls allow you to tailor your family's access to AOL on a screen-name-by-screen-name basis.

Note Parents should be sure that junior members of the family have access to only their own screen names. Each screen name requires a separate password; each password should be unique and carefully safeguarded. If someone else has your password, that person can pose as you, and you will be held responsible for his or her actions. If those actions violate AOL's rules, AOL can cancel your membership, and the whole family is out of luck.

Choosing Screen Names

Think about it for a second. AOL has over 22 million members now, and each of those members may have seven screen names. That's over 154 million possible screen names on AOL! Consider that every one of those screen names has to be unique, and the problems become absolutely mind-boggling. Devising an absolutely unique screen name can be quite a creative challenge, and finding out that the wonderfully imaginative name you cooked up has already been used by someone else can be the height of frustration.

Following are some additional screen name limitations:

- All screen names can contain between 3 and 16 characters (including spaces).
- All screen names must begin with a letter, rather than a number. (AOL automatically capitalizes the first letter in the name.)
- Screen names may be any combination of numbers and letters, but punctuation marks and symbols such as & can't be used.

- Screen names may contain any combination of upper- and lowercase letters, and AOL always displays your name the way you first typed it. However, screen names are not case sensitive or space sensitive. There's only one John Doe, so whether your friends address their e-mail to John Doe or johndoe, it will still arrive at your doorstep.
- Screen names are the property of AOL and are only yours to use for as long as you continue to be a member.

For a complete set of screen name guidelines, click the My AOL icon and choose Screen Names and then click More About Screen Names in the resulting window.

Setting Passwords

Passwords are the key to your account. Use the hints in the following list to make sure that your password is memorable, but difficult to copy or guess.

- **Make your password *longer* rather than *shorter*:** Long passwords are more difficult to guess than short ones.
- **Make your password cryptic:** Passwords should not contain easy-to-guess information about you or your family members (don't use the name of the family dog, for instance).
- **Make your password memorable (to you):** A reasonable substitute for totally random passwording is to choose the initials of an easy-to-remember phrase, such as "Four score and seven years ago . . ." (FSASYA), and intersperse it with numbers, such as F4SAS7YA. We don't recommend this particular example, though, as the phrase is much too well known, and you should never use passwords you've seen in examples. Choose a line from a favorite poem or song and make sure the numbers are unrelated to the phrase.

Tip

You probably will want to write down your password in case you forget it. If you do, be sure it's in a secure place. People have a way of losing their daily planners, and if you write the password on a sticky note and put it on your computer monitor or hide it under your keyboard, you may as well not use a password at all.

You choose and set your first password when you sign up to AOL initially. After that, follow these steps to change a password:

1. Sign on to AOL.
2. Click the My AOL icon and then choose Passwords. The Change Your AOL Password screen appears. (Alternatively, you can use Keyword: **Password** to reach this screen.)
3. Click the Change Password button, and the Change Your Password dialog box, shown in Figure 1-2, appears.

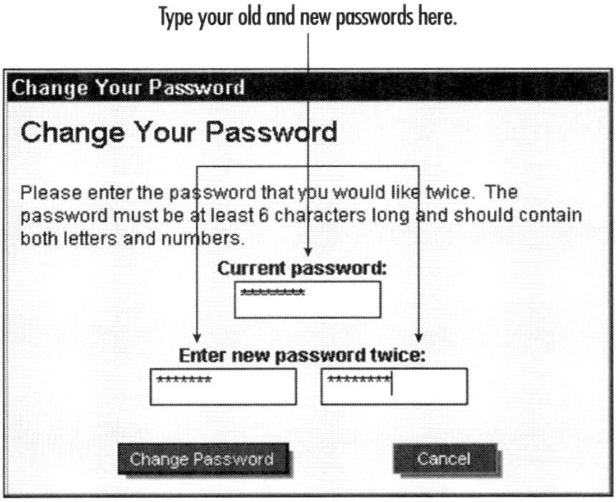

Figure 1-2. Changing a password requires knowing the old password.

4. Type your old password where prompted. This "old" password is the one you're currently using.
5. Type your new password in the appropriate text boxes. You'll be asked to type the new password twice, to be sure there are no errors. Each character you type appears as an asterisk on-screen to protect your password from anyone who may be looking over your shoulder.
6. Click the Change Password button, and your new password goes into effect immediately.

Getting Online

After your initial installation session, where you choose your master screen name and password, you'll want to know how to get online with AOL on a regular basis. You'll be happy to know that it is easy to get online, or "sign on." To do so, simply run your AOL software, choose the screen name you want to sign on with from the Select Screen Name menu, type your password, and click Sign On. AOL takes everything from there.

Finding Help in All the Right Places

Searching for the entry ramp to the AOL information superhighway? Pullover and stop for directions! If you're offline (not signed on to America Online) and unable to connect to America Online, you can get offline help. If you are able to get online, you'll find plenty of help resources there.

Offline Help

Your AOL software comes complete with a set of help databases that you can access whether you're connected to the service or not. To find them on Windows, run your software and choose Offline Help from the Help menu or press the F1 key on your keyboard. On the Mac, choose AOL Guide from the Help menu or press +?.

AOL also provides toll-free telephone support for general and technical questions. Representatives are available at 800-827-6364 or 703-448-8700 from 6 a.m. to 4 a.m. Eastern time, seven days a week. Before you call, have the following information handy in case it is needed: your screen name, your account address and phone number, and a detailed description of your problem. The first two items assume you already have an account; if you don't, just be prepared to explain your problem.

Online Help

A variety of helpful resources are available on AOL, and they're all yours for the taking. If you prefer to read, you'll find plenty of articles and message boards on virtually every AOL topic. If you benefit more by speaking to someone else, real-time help is available with member service representatives one-on-one or in help rooms. If you learn best with a teacher, you can even take a class on how to use AOL.

The first time you sign on, AOL greets you with a hearty welcome and an offer to learn more about AOL through the

Welcome to AOL 5.0 window. New members looking for more information will appreciate the guide for new members at Keyword: **QuickStart**. The resulting AOL QuickStart window (see Figure 1-3) concentrates on general features of the AOL service, rather than specific features of the AOL 5.0 software.

Figure 1-3. Get up to speed on AOL.

AOL Help is the main repository of help information online. In fact, we would go so far as to call it an online guide to AOL, authored by AOL itself. AOL Help is accessible in several ways: Click the AOL Help button in the bottom-right corner of the Welcome screen, choose Member Services Online Help from the Help menu, or use Keyword: **Help**.

You can also ask other AOL members for help. Members Helping Members is a community of members who gather to exchange and share information on AOL. To access the Members Helping Members message boards (message boards are discussed in Chapter 5), use Keyword: **MHM** and click the Message Board button at the top of the Members Helping Members window.

In addition to the various help resources we've already discussed, AOL has free, interactive classes on a variety of AOL-related topics, including Basic AOL, Intermediate AOL, Advanced AOL, and Basic Internet. You can get more information, class schedules, and the registration form at Keyword: **Help Class**.

AOL Member Perks and Services

AOL has many special offers and services for its members — everthing from long distance phone service to a personal reminder service. You can find out about the perks and services available by clicking the Favorites icon on the toolbar and selecting Member Exclusives from the drop-down menu. You notice that this selection brings up yet another menu containing a list of the offers and services available. Among the items on this list, you find the following:

- AOL Member Perks
- Long Distance Phone Service
- AOL Personal Reminder Service
- AOL Visa Card

Click one of the menu items to reach a window that describes the selected service or special offer. Then follow the on-screen cues to make the exclusive offer work for you!

Chapter 2

Getting to Know the AOL 5.0 Windows

In This Chapter

- Discover the AOL Welcome screen
- Learn how to navigate windows and use the toolbar
- Getting around with keywords, links, and URLs
- Protect your family and personal information

The starting point for your online adventures with America Online is the AOL Welcome screen. In this chapter, we show you how to make your way around this and other AOL screens by clicking buttons and icons, following links, and typing keywords and URLs.

And whenever you think about starting a new online adventure, your mind is likely to drift toward safety concerns. Is the online destination site safe? How can you protect your family? So before you venture out onto the streets of America Online, we want to tell you what the folks at AOL are doing to make sure your visit is safe and enjoyable.

Looking Over the AOL Welcome Screen

From the moment you sign on to the moment you sign off, AOL's Welcome screen stays with you, in one form or other. By design, it's one window you can never totally banish from your AOL experience. You can minimize it to a small box at the bottom of your AOL window, but it will never be far from your reach (see Figure 2-1).

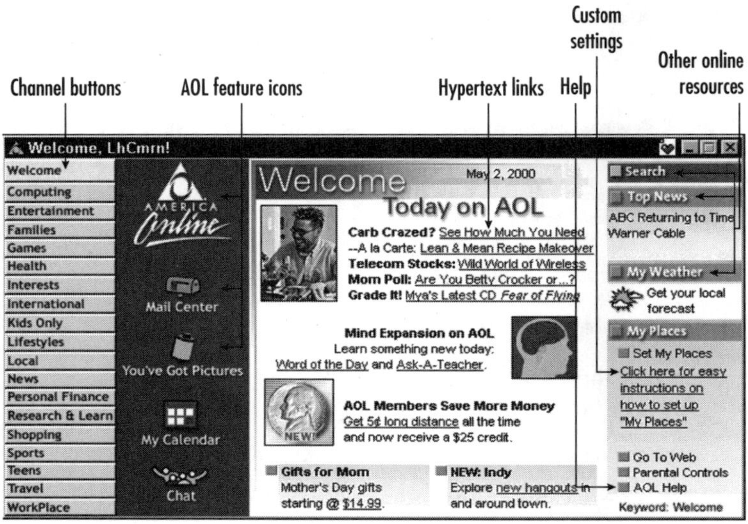

Figure 2-1. The AOL Welcome screen in all its glory.

The Welcome screen offers a wide variety of useful information and services intended to make your AOL experience as enjoyable and productive as possible. Along its left-hand side is an array of buttons that open the channel of your choice. Right next to the channel buttons is a row of large icons for major AOL features such as the Mail Center, You've Got Pictures, My Calendar, and Chat. The center of the Welcome screen is packed with hypertext links and buttons that lead to the day's hot topics and useful features. Finally, down the right-hand side of the screen are buttons that lead to customizing and outreach features: AOL Search, Top News, your local weather report, My Places, Parental Controls, the World Wide Web, and AOL Help.

My Places, a group of useful AOL and Internet sites you can customize on your own, made its Welcome screen debut in AOL 5.0. To customize My Places, click the Set My Places button on the Welcome screen. Now use the drop-down menus to select the five places you'd like to see on your Welcome screen, and click Save My Changes.

Navigating Through All the Options

In this section, we take a look at the menus, toolbar, and navigation bar that help you get around AOL.

Menus

Five quiet little phrases stretch across the top of the AOL window: File, Edit, Window, Sign Off, and Help. Each one represents a drop-down menu chock-full of useful functions and features. Click any one of them to open its menu and then click the desired menu item. The following descriptions and tables tell you what those menus offer (see Figure 2-2).

Figure 2-2. The AOL menu bar, toolbar, and navigation bar.

The File menu gives you many selections — familiar to any experienced computer user — for opening, closing, saving, printing, and otherwise working with the many types of files you run across while online. The following table lists some of the menu options and what they do.

File Menu Option	What It Does
New	Opens a blank text document that you can use for word processing
Open	Opens many kinds of text, graphic, audio, and HTML documents stored on your hard disk
Open Picture Gallery	Helps you quickly find one of the many images that you've saved

Continued

File Menu Option	What It Does
Close (Mac)	Closes a window
Save and Save As	Saves the e-mail, graphics, and contents of articles and Web pages you're currently viewing on your hard drive
Save to Personal Filing Cabinet	Saves e-mail to your Personal Filing Cabinet (which is custom-made for storing e-mail)
The Save to... (Mac)	Saves changes based on the active window (that is, an active window with a heart icon shows Save to Favorite Places on the menu)
Print Setup and Print	Helps you set up and print to the printer that is attached to your computer
Revert (Mac)	Discards any changes you made to a previously saved file that is open on your screen, allowing you to revert to the file's original state
Exit (Windows) and Quit (Mac)	One way to close the America Online software

The Edit menu is your helper whenever you're writing or viewing text and images on AOL. For example, you can copy and paste text into an e-mail message, spell check your e-mail, and so on.

The Window menu helps you organize, modify, and find the windows that tend to fill up your AOL screen. The following table shows some of the Windows menu options and what they do.

Window Menu Option	What It Does
Cascade	Arranges all open windows like a stack of playing cards
Tile	Arranges open windows side-by-side, like a mosaic floor
Arrange Icons	Organizes any minimized windows

Window Menu Option	What It Does
Clean Up Windows (Mac)	Stacks the windows like playing cards
Add Top Window to Favorite Places	Creates a shortcut to whatever the top window happens to be (see Chapter 6)

If you have modified dimensions of a window and/or moved it to a new position on the screen, you may find the following commands dealing with window size and location to be quite useful. At the bottom of the Windows menu is a listing of all currently open windows. Just click the window's name to bring it to the front, where you can see it.

The Sign Off menu offers two powerful choices when you are online:

- Switch Screen Name, which is available only when you are online, lets you switch to another screen name on your account without signing off.
- Sign Off is a bit different from Exit (Windows) or Quit (Mac) because it signs you off from AOL without closing the AOL software. If you sign on and off of AOL frequently, using this option is a huge time-saver.

When you are offline, the Sign Off menu is called Sign On.

The Help menu (need we say more?) offers assistance regardless of whether you are signed on to AOL. The following table outlines some of this menu's helpful options.

Help Menu Option	What It Does
Offline Help (Windows)	Accesses AOL's help database stored on your hard drive
AOL Guide (Mac)	Accesses AOL's help database stored on your hard drive
Help Center (Mac)	Links to the Mac OS Help Center
Show Balloons (Mac)	Turns on the Mac's Balloon Help system
What's New in AOL 5.0	Explains AOL's newest features (Keyword: **Click and Go**)

Unlike the Help menu for most computer programs, this Help menu connects you to online resources such as Member Services Online, Parental Controls, Accounts and Billing, and AOL Access Phone Numbers. The Windows Help menu also offers an About America Online command, which provides information about AOL and your computer that the folks at AOL Technical Support may want to know, should you need to call them for assistance. (On the Mac, this command is under the Apple menu.)

Toolbar

Right below the AOL menus is the AOL toolbar, a row of icons that conceal even more drop-down menus (see Figure 2-3). The toolbar is a very powerful feature of AOL, and you'll be moving your mouse in its direction throughout your online travels. At the left, you find four icons dedicated (mostly) to e-mail: Read, Write, Mail Center, and Print. Next come My Files, My AOL, and Favorites. As the names imply, these menus are the center of your personalized AOL experience. They provide access to information stored on your computer, open AOL features that have been customized to your needs, and offer shortcuts to your favorite places on AOL and the Web. Internet is a menu of useful Internet-related features. Channels is an alternative route to AOL's channels, which are also available through the Welcome screen. People offers AOL's features for chat and member interaction. Quotes takes stock market fans to Quotes and Portfolios. Perks goes to the special offers at AOL Member Perks. Calendar opens My Calendar, your own personal appointment calendar.

Navigation Bar

The navigation bar is located right below the toolbar and contains some powerful features for getting around AOL and the Web (refer to Figure 2-3). The basic features of the toolbar will already be familiar to those of you who know how to use a Web browser, but AOL has gone one step further by extending its functions to areas within AOL. Features of the navigation bar, from left to right, include the following:

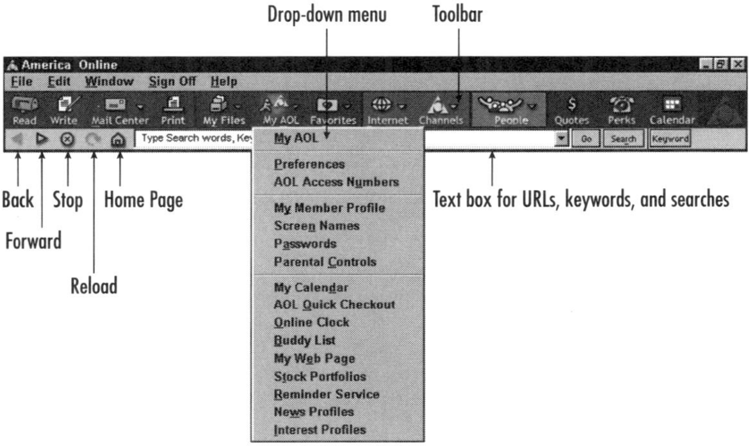

Figure 2-3. AOL's handy tools for getting around online.

- **Back, Forward, Stop, Reload, and Home Page buttons:** Move you backward and forward through AOL windows or Web pages you've previously viewed (provided those windows are still open); stop the loading process — primarily for Web pages — which can be a real time-saver if you know that you've gone to the wrong page; reload a Web page (in case it gets stuck during loading); and take you to AOL's home page on the Web, AOL.com.
- **Text box:** Gives you a place to type search words, keywords, or Web addresses. After typing, click the Go button, press the Enter key, or click the Search button. AOL opens the desired AOL area or Web page, or performs a search. If you click the down arrow icon next to the text box, you reveal the History Trail — a list of the last 25 areas or Web pages you visited. To return to any item on the list, just click the item you want in the drop-down list.

- **Search and Keyword buttons:** Open the AOL Search window and AOL's Keyword entry window, respectively. Just type a keyword or search word into the white text box on the navigation bar (described in this section), press the Enter key, and you'll have your results in a matter of moments.

Tip

The far right-hand side of the AOL toolbar holds one item that couldn't fit on the navigation bar — the AOL Progress icon — which is a version of the triangular AOL logo. When you're loading an AOL page or Web page, the icon swirls to show you that the requested page is on its way. When the page has finished loading, the icon stops its animated motion.

Hypertext Links

Hypertext links are a wondrous thing, because they're one of the features that make the World Wide Web the wonder that it is today. Hypertext links are words that work like buttons. They can perform actions, such as opening new windows or Web pages. You can identify a hyperlink in several ways. First, hyperlinks are almost always colored bright blue, and the text is underlined. You will find some exceptions to this rule. Regardless, if you move the mouse pointer over a suspected hyperlink, it should turn into the familiar pointing hand. One click on a hyperlink takes you wherever the hyperlink leads, and once you've clicked a hyperlink, it changes color to indicate that you've already clicked it.

Since hyperlinks can lead almost anywhere (good or bad), it pays to look before you click. Windows members can see where a particular hyperlink leads by moving the mouse pointer over a hyperlink or button on the Web page. A small caption may appear telling you the destination of the link. Mac members can see where a Web hyperlink leads by holding down the Option key while single-clicking a hyperlink, and then choosing Edit Address from the resulting context menu. To see where an AOL hyperlink leads, press the Option key and single-click the address. A small window appears and displays the hyperlink's destination. If you don't see the link's destination, look at the bottom border of the page's window. It may display the address or description of that button or hyperlink.

Discovering Keywords and URLs

The shortest route between two points is a straight line, and when you want to go somewhere on AOL, there's no line straighter than a keyword. *Keywords* are individual words or short phrases that can take you almost anywhere on the AOL service. When you know an online area's keyword, you can stop clicking link after link in order to get there — just type the keyword. You can type it into the text box on the navigation bar and press the Enter key. Alternatively, you can click the Keyword button on the navigation bar, type the keyword into the Keyword window (see Figure 2-4), and click the Go button.

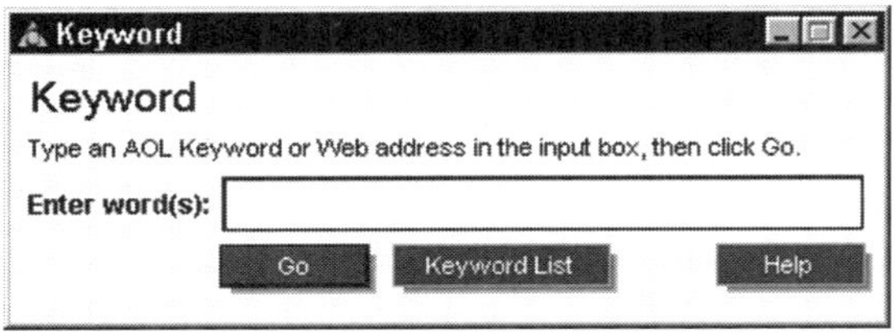

Figure 2-4. The Keyword window — just type the keyword and click Go.

Your next stop is your desired destination. Keywords work only on AOL — for areas operated by AOL and its partners — but at last count, there were over 15,000 AOL keywords providing shortcuts to everything from **AA** (American Airlines) to **ZOO**.

How do you find keywords? Try one of the following:

- When you arrive at an online area you like, look around and see if a keyword is listed in the window.
- Visit Keyword: **Keyword.**
- Click the Keyword List button in the Keyword window.
- Guess. Keywords are often easy to guess. If you guess wrong, AOL may even suggest keywords that will work for you.

Note: If you try a keyword and a window opens informing you that the keyword was not found, don't worry. If AOL cannot find a keyword, it automatically initiates an AOL Search for you and displays the results in the window that opened. If you simply misspelled the keyword, AOL provides a hyperlink in the window that lets you enter the keyword again.

URLs are addresses on the World Wide Web. You see them everywhere these days, in advertisements, on business cards, and embroidered on people's shirtsleeves. URL stands for Universal Resource Locator, and it looks like this: `http://www.aol.com` (which is the URL to AOL's home page on the World Wide Web). You can use a URL just like you use a keyword. Type it into the text box on the navigation bar or enter it into the Keyword window. In moments, the corresponding Web page should open right before your eyes.

Setting Up Safeguards

America Online has over 22 million members, making it the size of a very large metropolis. Knowing this, you can probably surmise the importance of safety online. AOL also recognizes the need for community safety and offers the Neighborhood Watch area (Keyword: **Neighborhood Watch**) to help safeguard and educate its membership.

We've prepared a list of top ten advisories to protect you and safeguard your account. Read them, live them, love them. They will save you, your account, and your sanity.

1. Devise complicated passwords for each of your screen names. Make your passwords as long as possible (at least six characters, preferably eight) and use a combination of numbers and letters. See Chapter 1 for more password creation tips.
2. Protect your password like the crown jewels. Never divulge your password to anyone online, no matter who they claim they are or what disaster they claim just happened. The AOL staff will never ask for your password.
3. Make quick password recoveries. If you or a member of your family accidentally gives out a password, change it and all other passwords on your account immediately at Keyword: **Password**.
4. Keep private information private. Don't put your street address in member profiles or tell just anyone your phone number. Be on your guard about divulging information in children's member profiles. Be wary of listing geographic locations, school names, or any other identifying information.

5. Lock your mailbox with AOL's mail controls (at Keyword: **Mail Controls**). Use the feature to block all e-mail you or members of your family do not want to receive.
6. Never download files attached to e-mail unless you know specifically what the files contain and trust the person who sent them.
7. Don't believe everything you read in e-mail. Be skeptical of free offers, wild claims, or anything that seems too good or bad to believe.
8. Protect your information on the Internet. Not all Web sites have a commitment to protecting your privacy as AOL does. Look for a privacy policy and read it before divulging any private information.
9. Talk to your children about what is and isn't okay to talk about online. Teach them not to give out any personal information or their password, and to come to you if someone does ask for any information that makes them uncomfortable.
10. Report problems to AOL. Use Keyword: **Notify AOL** anytime you're online to file a report.

Terms of Service

AOL's Terms of Service (which most of us shorten to the acronym TOS) contain America Online's commitments to its members, as well as the members' rights and responsibilities to the AOL community. AOL organizes its Terms of Service into three sections: the Member Agreement, the Community Guidelines, and the Privacy Policy. AOL prides itself on offering all three in straightforward, easy-to-understand language. Although we don't want to reprint the Terms of Service in this book (they do change from time to time, after all), we strongly encourage you to read them.

Definition

AOL is a community, and it has a set of guidelines for what goes on in its community. AOL calls these rules the Terms of Service. All AOL members agree to abide by these terms when they sign up for their accounts with AOL. Do you know what the terms entail? If not, take a moment now to visit Keyword: **TOS** and read the terms in their entirety.

Notify AOL

After you know what is acceptable and unacceptable behavior online, you are in a better position to notice inappropriate behavior by someone else. If you are confronted with such behavior, do what you'd do in your community — notify the authorities. In this case, that's AOL, and you can report a problem at Notify AOL, which is accessible via Keyword: **Notify AOL**.

Notify AOL lets you report violations that occur in the following areas: chats, e-mail (and attachments), Instant Messages, message boards, Web pages, and screen names/profiles. Just click the appropriate button on the left-hand side of the Notify AOL window for the report form. Fill in the information as requested (the more information you provide, the more likely action can be taken). In most cases, you'll need to demonstrate the problem, and that often requires pasting a copy of the violation into the Notify AOL window. If you're unfamiliar with this technique, click the How to Copy & Paste button in the lower-left corner of the Notify AOL screen.

Parental Controls

Dave is the proud father of a bright seven-year-old who feels at home on computers, and it is only a matter of time before she gets online and asks for her own screen name. Dave is concerned about the safety of his daughter. Will she receive inappropriate e-mail? Download files from people she doesn't know? Fall prey to scams in Instant Messages? Or venture into dangers on the Internet? Children are particularly vulnerable online and deserve the care and attention of their parents to protect them.

Thankfully, AOL recognizes the needs of parents and children. AOL offers what it calls Parental Controls, a set of tools that allow or restrict access to various parts of the AOL service. While Parental Controls don't eliminate the need for parents to sit down with their kids and experience AOL together, they do give kids the freedom and security for independent explorations. And they give parents peace of mind!

Tip

Upon opening the Parental Controls window, AOL presents you with an array of choices. We recommend taking a moment to watch the slideshow about the features and benefits of using Parental Controls. The slideshow starts automatically; if you don't want it to play, just click the Pause button.

Follow these steps to set up parental controls for your child's screen name:

1. Click the My AOL icon and choose Parental Controls or go to Keyword: **Parental Controls.** The AOL Parental Controls window opens, as shown in Figure 2-5.

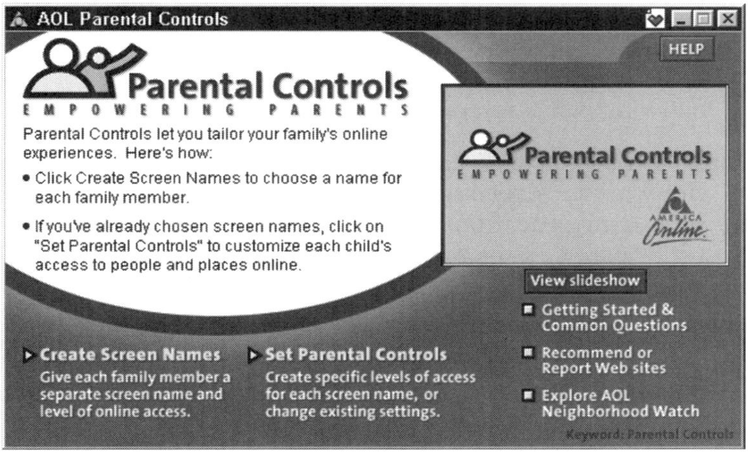

Figure 2-5. Parents are empowered with Parental Controls.

Note: To get started with Parental Controls, you need a screen name to control. All parental control settings are tied to individual screen names. If your child doesn't yet have a screen name, you can create one by clicking Create Screen Names in the lower-left corner of the Parental Controls window. Remember that you need to be signed on with a master screen name to create a new screen name.

2. Click Set Parental Controls in the lower center of the AOL Parental Controls window. Another window appears and shows a list of the custom controls and current settings.
3. Click the down arrow to the right of the Edit Controls For field at the top of the window and choose your child's screen name from the drop-down list. The list of custom controls in the window is updated to show the current settings for that screen.

Note: The small icon of a person next to a screen name in the drop-down list denotes that the name is designated as a master screen name. As long as you are using a master screen name, you can edit any of the screen names on the account.

4. Click the square icon next to the custom control you want to change. A customization window appears and offers you an explanation of the settings along with option buttons or check boxes for your choices.
5. Click the option button or check box next to the appropriate setting for the screen name you selected in Step 3.
6. Click Save to save your new settings or Cancel to close the window without saving the new settings.

The following paragraphs discuss each of the custom controls.

E-Mail Control: Mail controls let you determine limits on how, and with whom, a screen name can send and receive e-mail. The first three settings near the top of the window allow for general, across-the-board control. You can decide whether the screen name can exchange e-mail with all AOL and Internet addresses (Allow all E-Mail), exchange e-mail only with other AOL members, or block all e-mail entirely.

The next three settings let you allow (or block) specific e-mail domains and addresses. You can allow e-mail only from AOL members and the specific domains and addresses you select, allow e-mail only from listed AOL and Internet domains and addresses, or block e-mail from listed AOL and Internet domains and addresses. You can list the specific domains and addresses you wish to allow or block by typing them in the top field on the right and clicking the Add button.

At the bottom of the Mail Controls window is the file attachments setting. If you don't want the screen name to receive e-mail with attached files or pictures, be sure that this setting is enabled.

Chat Control: Chat rooms can be particularly scary places for kids. These real-time conversations are often a little too fast and furious for young readers, and you never know who your kids may meet. AOL offers several settings to empower parents to control access to chat rooms.

You can block three kinds of chat rooms: All People Connection chat areas, all non-AOL-sanctioned chat areas, and all the rest of the chat areas. You can select just one setting, or block access to all chat areas by selecting the top three settings.

Note: The fourth setting at the bottom of the Chat Control window lets you block hyperlinks in chat rooms. Blocking these hyperlinks is strongly recommended for screen names of any young family member who may click a hyperlink without first knowing where it leads. Such an action can result in giving out personal or billing information to the people who will compromise it.

IM Control: Instant Messages are real-time, one-on-one notes that members can pass back and forth. The Instant Message controls are simple: You can either allow Instant Messages or block them.

Web Control: The Internet is a worldwide network of computers, offering rich resources for kids but also adult content that's inappropriate for kids. Web controls let you restrict access to sites based on age.

Additional Master Screen Names Control: You can designate other screen names on your account as master screen names. This allows the users associated with those names to create, delete, and restore screen names, change an account's billing options, and edit the majority of parental control settings. Only screen names set for the General Access category can be designated as master screen names.

Download Control: Download controls let you block the ability of a user of a particular screen name to download files from AOL software libraries and/or FTP sites.

Newsgroup Control: Newsgroup controls let you restrict access to newsgroups, which are discussion areas on the Internet. They can be adult in nature or contain inappropriate language.

Premium Services Control: Don't want your little angel playing Air Warrior after school? Block premium services and prevent your monthly bill from skyrocketing.

Parental Control Categories: If you're in a hurry or don't need such minute control over a screen name's access, you can click one of the general category buttons arrayed along the bottom of the main Parental Controls window. Changing a category resets all custom controls to that category's settings. There are settings appropriate for adults, Mature Teens, Young Teens, and Kids Only.

Chapter 3

Communicating Through E-mail

In This Chapter

- Discover the world of electronic mail
- Learn how to access, read, and reply to your e-mail
- Create, check, and format your e-mail
- Save and organize your e-mail
- Find out how to insert graphics and attach files

E-mail is an electronic, private communication. You will assuredly receive e-mail as an AOL member, and almost definitely send it. E-mail is easy: no paper, no pens, no stamps, no fuss. E-mail is convenient: You can use it wherever you are on AOL. Even better, e-mail costs nothing beyond your normal AOL connect charges.

Every screen name on your AOL account has an online mailbox where the e-mail you've received and sent is temporarily held. And because you can have up to seven screen names on your AOL account, you can also have up to seven mailboxes, each of which can hold up to 1,000 pieces of e-mail.

An Overview of the Mail Center

We start the e-mail discussion by introducing the AOL Mail Center. Actually, AOL has two things called *Mail Center*. One is the icon on your toolbar and its menu. The other is a window accessible through the first menu item in your Mail Center menu. You can see both the Mail Center menu and the Mail Center window in Figure 3-1.

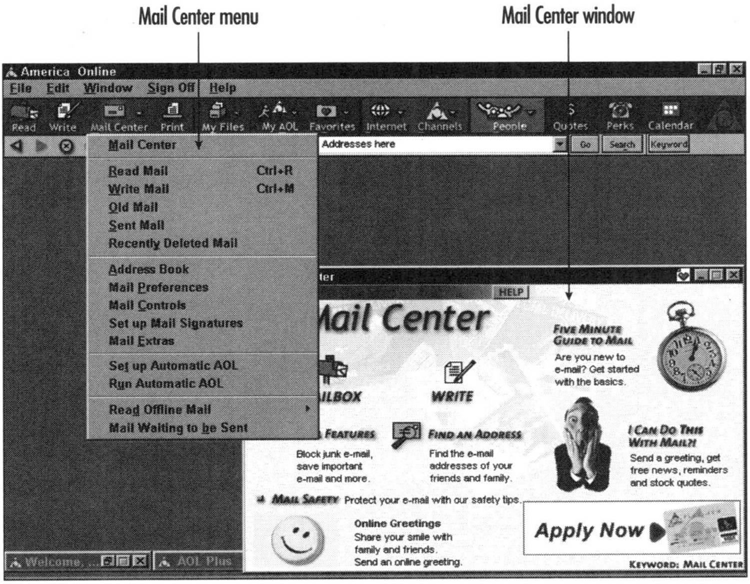

Figure 3-1. Use the Mail Center menu item to open the Mail Center window.

The Mail Center menu offers easy access to the most common e-mail features. The following table outlines the menu options and what they do.

Mail Center Menu Option	What It Does
Mail Center	Opens the Mail Center window
Read Mail	Opens or refreshes your mailbox (list of new e-mail)
Write Mail	Opens a Write Mail window (for composing a new e-mail message)
Old Mail	Opens or refreshes your old e-mail list
Sent Mail	Opens or refreshes your list of sent e-mail
Recently Deleted Mail	Displays all e-mail you deleted in the last 24 hours (a new feature in AOL 5.0)

Mail Center Menu Option	What It Does
Address Book	Stores and manages e-mail addresses
Mail Preferences	Helps you set e-mail options (spell checking, quoting style, and so on)
Mail Controls	Helps you stop junk mail and set parental controls
Mail Extras	Adds pizzazz (banners, greeting cards, smileys, and so on) to your e-mail
Set Up Automatic AOL and Run Automatic AOL	Helps download and stores messages automatically
Read Offline Mail and Mail Waiting to Be Sent	Gives you offline access to incoming/saved e-mail or e-mail you've saved or marked to be sent later

Tip

We revisit saving e-mail later in the chapter, but for now you should know that you can choose Read Offline Mail and then select Incoming/Saved Mail from the submenu to see a list of e-mail you've already read.

The Mail Center window (really an entire area, shown in Figure 3-1) is a different beast from the Mail Center menu. Rather than providing access to popular e-mail features, it offers extra resources such as a tutorial on using e-mail. You can return to the Mail Center window with Keyword: **Mail Center**.

Receiving and Reading E-mail

First things first: Do you have e-mail to read? You can find out by signing on to AOL, turning up your sound volume, and listening for the "You've got mail!" announcement immediately after the "Welcome!" greeting. Another way to check for new e-mail is to look at your mailbox icon near the top left of the Welcome screen (or on the toolbar). If you have new e-mail, the red flag is raised on the icon.

All new members have e-mail from the moment they sign on. The good folks from America Online send you some. To open your mailbox, click either of the two mailbox icons or press Ctrl+R on Windows or ⌘+R on the Mac.

Scanning Your Online Mailbox

AOL lists all your e-mail in the center of your online mailbox window, as shown in Figure 3-2. Each line shows an icon, the date the e-mail was sent, the address (screen name) of the person who sent the e-mail, and the subject line (the topic of the e-mail). Across the top of the window are tabs for three types of mail: New Mail, Old Mail, and Sent Mail. Across the bottom are five buttons, starting with Read (which opens a piece of e-mail). The following sections tell you what happens when you use these buttons.

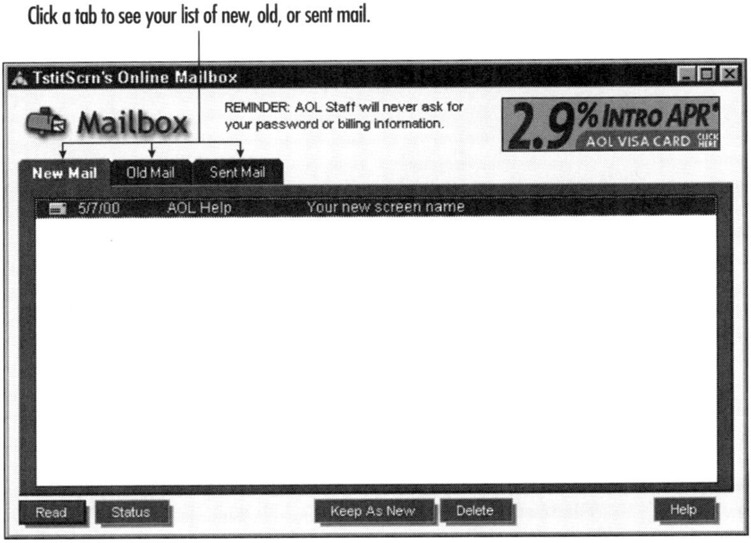

Figure 3-2. An Online Mailbox, complete with e-mail from AOL.

Reading Your New E-mail

To read an e-mail message, first make sure that the e-mail you want to open is selected (highlighted). If it isn't, place your pointer over it and click. Now click the Read button. Alternatively, you can double-click the e-mail you want to read. Your e-mail opens in a new window on your screen (see Figure 3-3).

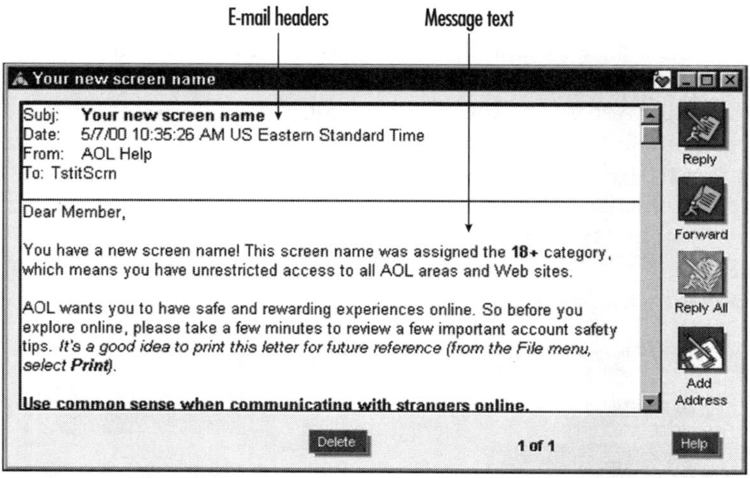

Figure 3-3. Your first e-mail comes from AOL.

The e-mail window has a bunch of buttons on it, too. The following list tells you what these buttons do:

- **Delete:** Removes the e-mail from your mailbox.

Tip You can retrieve deleted mail for up to 24 hours by choosing the Recently Deleted Mail function in the Mail Center menu, but we don't recommend you use the Delete button until you feel more comfortable working with e-mail.

- **Next:** Opens the next e-mail in your mailbox; the numbers to the left of Next tell you how much e-mail you have in your mailbox.

- **Reply:** Lets you send a response to the currently viewed e-mail message.

- **Forward:** Lets you forward the entire e-mail to another person.
- **Reply All:** Lets you send a response to all persons who received this e-mail. If only one person receives an e-mail, the button is grayed out for that particular message.
- **Add Address:** Lets you add the sender's address to your Address Book.
- **Help:** Leads to more help about using e-mail.

Recovering Deleted Mail

Have you ever accidentally deleted an e-mail? The Recently Deleted Mail menu selection (accessible under the Mail Center button on the toolbar), one of AOL 5.0's new features, lets you view all e-mail deleted in the past 24 hours and decide whether to keep it as new or permanently delete it.

This feature is an obvious benefit if you accidentally delete e-mail or change your mind. If you delete e-mail to remove it from your mailbox for privacy or security reasons, however, you must visit your Recently Deleted Mail list and permanently delete it. If you neglect to do this, your e-mail may remain accessible to someone else using your screen name (if that person has access to your password).

Understanding E-mail Addresses on AOL and the Internet

Just like regular mail—which requires names, street addresses, cities, states, zip codes, and sometimes countries to find its recipients—e-mail needs addresses. On AOL, your screen name is your e-mail address.

When you give your e-mail address to other AOL members, you can give them just your screen name. If someone who is not an AOL member asks for your address, you need to add `@aol.com` to the end of your screen name. When you send e-mail to someone on the Internet or post a message on a newsgroup, AOL automatically attaches this Internet e-mail form of your address.

Definition

Every Internet e-mail address has two components: the name and the domain. The name is similar to an AOL screen name, though it may be a bit longer or contain characters AOL screen names don't have. Everything before the @ symbol is the *name*. For example, in the address `authors@jenuine.net`, the name is `authors`. The *domain* is everything after the @ symbol. In this case, the domain is `jenuine.net`.

Creating, Sending, Replying, and Forwarding

Before you can send e-mail, you must first compose it. You can do any of the following to bring up the Write Mail window (see Figure 3-4):

- Click the Write icon on the toolbar.
- Choose the Mail Center icon and then choose Write Mail.
- Press Ctrl+M (Windows) or +M (Mac).

Tip

The Write Mail window on Windows and the Mac differs in small ways. The biggest difference is the Send To and Copy To fields in the window. Windows has both of these fields, while the Mac only has a Send To field — but the Mac's single field has the capability to send regular mail, courtesy copies, and blind courtesy copies with a handy drop-down menu.

Use the following steps to compose an e-mail message in the Write Mail window:

1. Click in the Send To field (the first field in the Write Mail window) and type the intended recipient's address. Then press the Tab key on your keyboard to move the cursor to the next field (on Windows, the next field is the Copy To field).
2. Type an e-mail address in the Copy To field if you want to send a courtesy copy of your message to that address. You may also leave this field blank. Press Tab again, and your cursor should be in the Subject field.

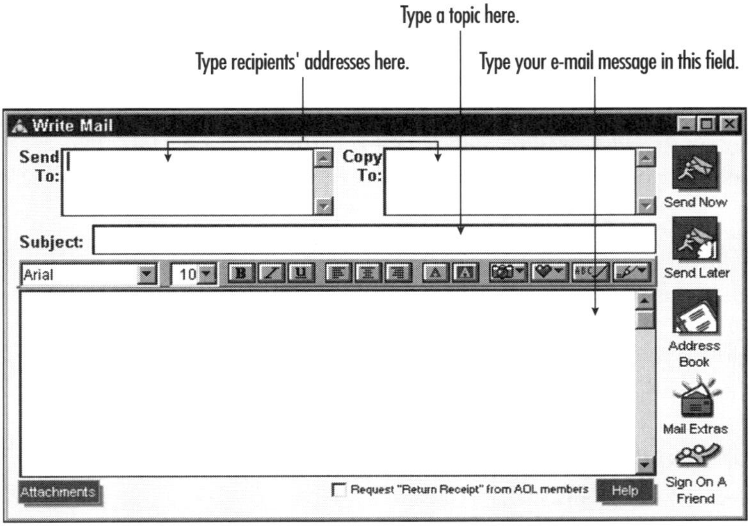

Figure 3-4. Compose your e-mail in the Write Mail window.

On the Mac, there is no Copy To field — instead, you designate a courtesy copy be sent to a particular screen name by choosing CC from the drop-down menu to the left of the screen name.

3. Type the topic of your e-mail in the Subject field. Make your subject line as informative as it can be; otherwise your recipient may mistake your message for junk e-mail and delete it. Press Tab again to reach the last and largest text field, which holds your e-mail message.
4. Type your message into the large text field.
5. Once you've finished composing your e-mail, check your e-mail carefully. Did you type the screen name exactly as it should be? Did you say everything you wanted? Is your spelling correct?
6. When your e-mail is ready to go, click the Send Now button in the upper-right corner of the window. AOL responds by instantly sending your e-mail, closing the e-mail window, and confirming that your e-mail was sent.

Replying to E-mail

Except for the times you initiate a correspondence, much of the e-mail you send will likely be replies to e-mail that you've received. And all the e-mail you read has a Reply button on it. If you've already read an e-mail and it is no longer in your New Mail list, you can click the Old Mail tab and open it from there.

The Reply button appears in the top-right corner of the e-mail window. Click it, and a new compose e-mail window appears, complete with the sender's address in the Send To field and a subject (preceded by *Re:* which stands for *Reply*) in the subject field. To dash off a reply now, you only need to type your message in the message field and click Send Now as usual.

Forwarding E-mail

Forwarding is simply sending an entire copy of the e-mail you received to someone else, who may or may not be the person who sent it to you originally. When you come across an e-mail you feel would be best served by forwarding it, just click the Forward button on the right side of the window (below Reply). AOL responds by opening a new e-mail window.

You'll notice that AOL fills in the subject line and prefixes it with *Fwd:* which stands for *Forward*. To complete the forward, type in the appropriate addresses and any message you feel necessary to explain why you're forwarding the e-mail. Click Send Now, and off it goes! When your recipient opens the forwarded e-mail, he or she first sees your message (if you included one) and then a copy of the forwarded e-mail below that, complete with e-mail headers.

Checking the Status of Your Sent Mail

Did your e-mail reach its destination? To check the status of an e-mail you've sent, select Sent Mail from the Mail Center menu, select the e-mail you want to check, and click the Status button at the bottom of the window.

The status window lists the address(es) to which your e-mail was sent, along with a status beside each address. If the recipient read your e-mail, a date and time appears to the right of that person's address. If the e-mail hasn't been read, you'll see "(not yet read)." Two other status messages you may see are "you cannot check status of Internet mail" (which appears for all Internet addresses), and "ignored."

Attaching Files

Remember that Attachments button (Windows) or the Attach Files button (Mac) in the Write Mail window? Clicking it produces the Attachments window (see Figure 3-5) through which you can attach (and detach) one or more files.

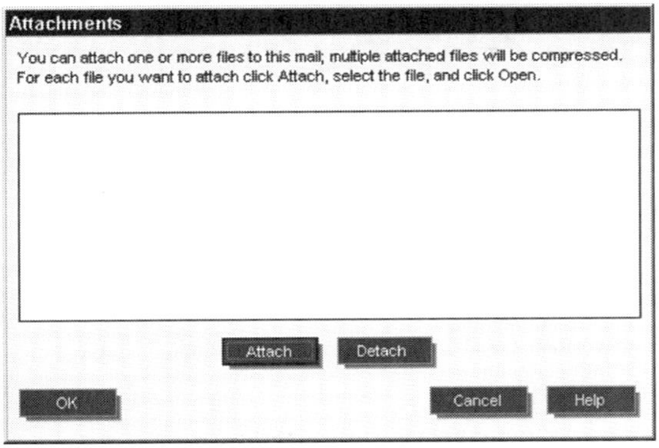

Figure 3-5. Use this window to attach files to your e-mail.

To attach files in Windows, click the Attach button, locate the file in the standard find file window, and click Open. Your Attachments window now reflects the attached file, denoted by the file's address and name on your hard drive. Repeat to add another file.

To attach files on the Mac, click the Attach Files button, locate the file in the Open File window, and click Enclose. The file's name appears in the Attachments field of your e-mail window. Repeat the process if you want to add more files. If you want to Detach files, select the name of the file you want to remove in the Attachments field and click Detach Files.

When you're finished attaching files in Windows, click OK in the lower-left corner of the Attachments window. Then complete the e-mail as you normally would. In your message, we recommend that you reference the attached file for your recipients, telling them what the file contains, any special software they may need to use or view it, and so on. When your e-mail is ready, click the Send Now button.

Definition

If you attached multiple files, AOL responds with a message that it is compressing your attachments, which means it is decreasing the size of the files by using ZIP (Windows) or SIT (Mac) file compression techniques and then archiving them into one file for transfer.

Saving and Organizing Your E-mail

Don't make the mistake of thinking your e-mail will stay in your online mailbox forever. Within a few days, the e-mail you've read disappears, and the e-mail you've sent disappears after about a month. Why? AOL stores that e-mail on its own computers, and space is at a premium. If you want to keep track of your online correspondence, you're going to have to use space on your own hard disk. And the best way to do this is with your Personal Filing Cabinet.

Definition

The *Personal Filing Cabinet* (PFC) is AOL's built-in system for saving, organizing, and searching the e-mail you've read and sent. Each of the screen names on your account has its own PFC, and you can password-protect your PFC to hide its contents from prying eyes.

Although you can save e-mail to the PFC on an item-by-item basis, most folks prefer to automatically save all e-mail to the PFC. To do this, you need to change some AOL Mail Preferences as follows:

1. Click the My AOL icon and choose Preferences. The Preferences dialog box appears.
2. Click the Mail icon, and the Mail Preferences window appears.
3. Click in the appropriate check boxes to enable the options Retain All Mail I Send in My Personal Filing Cabinet and Retain All Mail I Read in My Personal Filing Cabinet.

On the Mac, these preferences are Save the Mail I Send and Save the Mail I Read. Setting these preferences affects all screen names on your account, so you have to do this only once.

4. Click OK to save your mail preference settings.

You can read what's in your Personal Filing Cabinet whether you're online or offline by clicking the My Files icon and choosing Personal Filing Cabinet. The buttons along the bottom of the Personal Filing Cabinet window let you open a selected e-mail, add or rename a folder, delete an item, configure Auto AOL, and search the PFC (using Find) for e-mail containing certain names, words, or phrases.

Aids for Creating, Checking, and Formatting Your E-mail

With just a touch more effort, you can elevate your e-mail from the gray, drab basics to a colorful, efficient communications tool.

Spell Checking

Not evriwon wood agre, butt spellin and grammer is verry importint two gud komyounicashuns. Fortunately for us, a spelling and grammar helper is built right into the AOL software. To start a spell check, click the Spell Check button in the Write Mail window (it's the one that has the letters ABC and a check mark on it).

The spell check begins wherever the text insertion mark happens to be, which can just as easily be at the end of a document as at the beginning. The spell checker starts looking for misspelled words, common typographical errors, and common grammatical errors. When it finds one, the Check Spelling window opens to display its findings.

Styled Text

Styled text is just another way to say formatting, a concept that is very familiar to anyone who uses a word processor. The AOL Write Mail window includes a formatting bar, which makes all this styling possible (refer to Figure 3-4). We don't have room to describe each styled text feature, but there's nothing wrong with experimenting on your own. Just open a Write Mail window, type a few sentences of sample text, highlight a bit of the text, and click a button or two on your formatting bar.

Signatures

Every screen name on your AOL account can have up to five signature files, which are stored on your hard disk. Signatures appear at the end of e-mails and can save you the time of adding your name and/or other information to each e-mail. To create your signatures, click the Mail Center icon on the AOL toolbar, select Set Up Signatures, and click the Create button.

Note While the Set Up Signatures window is open, you have the choice to edit or delete the sig(s) that you created, or declare one of your sigs as a default. Your default signature is automatically added to every e-mail you create with this screen name.

Inserting Pictures and Graphics

Why not send illustrated e-mail that includes a picture? AOL gives you the creative power to exchange fully illustrated e-mail with all your friends and family who use AOL. Build a family photo album or just a snapshot.

To insert a picture in your e-mail, start with an open Write Mail window and follow these steps:

1. Click the Insert a Picture button on the formatting bar. The Insert a Picture button is the one with the camera on it.
2. Choose Insert a Picture from the drop-down menu, and an Open window appears.
3. Browse through the available drives and folders to find the picture file you're looking for.
4. Click OK.

The photo is added to your e-mail!

Chapter 4

Other Communications Options

In This Chapter

- Discover how to exchange Instant Messages
- Keep tabs on family and friends with your Buddy List
- Converse online through chats and conferences
- Read and post on message boards and newsgroups
- Keep in touch with AOL Mail

Do you see your friends and family as often as you'd like? With AOL, you can chat with them in real time and at no additional cost. It's easy, quick, and simple. We can show you how through the use of Instant Messages, Buddy Lists, and chat and conference rooms.

After the heady rush of Instant Messages and chats, you may be ready for something a bit more down to earth. We have just the thing: message boards and newsgroups. Unlike Instant Messages and chats, which take place in real time, these message centers help you take things at your own pace.

Instant Messages

An Instant Message is a live, totally private, one-on-one chat session between two people who are currently online. The Instant Message (or IM) window doesn't take up a lot of space on your screen and doesn't interfere with any of your other online activities. With Instant Messages, you can do the following:

- Find out who's currently online and available to chat.
- Hold a private online conversation with selected people (even more than one at a time) in a chat room.
- Meet new people whose profiles you've seen in AOL's Member Directory.
- Use AOL Instant Messenger to exchange IMs with friends who aren't using AOL.
- Collaborate with your coworkers (even those in different locations) in real time.
- View a Web page simultaneously with your online friends by sharing hypertext links.

Sending and Receiving Instant Messages

It doesn't take much to start an Instant Message (IM) conversation. Follow these simple steps:

1. To open an IM window, click the People icon and choose Instant Message. The Send Instant Message dialog box opens, as shown in Figure 4-1.
2. Type your friend's screen name into the To box and type a greeting into the message box below it.
3. Click Send.

Figure 4-1. The Send Instant Message window — just add a name and a greeting, and click Send.

Note You can set up a member profile to tell a potential instant-messaging friend a little about yourself. Click the My AOL icon and choose My Member Profile, fill in the requested information, and click Update to save your profile.

If you receive an Instant Message and want to respond, follow these steps:

1. Click the Respond button. The Instant Message From window changes to provide a text entry box at the bottom for your reply.
2. Type your message in the bottom text entry box.
3. Click Send, and your IM friend will receive your response along with the usual chime.

Protecting Your Privacy and Personal Information

Unfortunately, not everyone who sends you an Instant Message is a friend. People who discover your screen name, or simply guess it at random, may use an IM to try to fool you into giving them important personal information, such as a credit card number or your AOL password. Nobody from AOL will ever ask you for your password or billing information online, and you should never share that information with anyone, no matter how official they may seem or what threats they make.

Tip: If you receive an Instant Message requesting personal information don't close it — click the Notify AOL button on AOL's Terms of Service window (Keyword: **TOS**) and follow the instructions.

Buddy List

The Buddy List is an essential tool for anyone who uses Instant Messages or chats online. You'll see a list of which friends and associates are currently online, and you'll see when they've signed on or signed off.

Your buddies are anyone you want them to be, provided they are AOL members or use AOL Instant Messenger (AIM). If you know a person's screen name(s) or AIM name, you can add it to your Buddy List.

To view your Buddy List Setup window, click the My AOL icon on the AOL toolbar and select Buddy List (or go to Keyword: **Buddy List**). Your Buddy List actually starts with three empty lists (or groups) called Buddies, Family, and Co-Workers, as shown in Figure 4-2. Follow these steps to immediately begin adding screen names to one of these three lists:

1. In the Buddy List Setup window, click a list to select it.
2. Click Edit at the bottom of the Setup window. The Edit Buddy List window appears and prompts you to enter a screen name.
3. Type the screen name of the buddy you want to add to your list and click Add Buddy. Your new buddy's screen name then appears in the Buddies in Group listing at the right of your Edit Buddy List window.
4. Repeat Step 3 to add additional screen names to this Buddy List group.
5. When you're finished adding screen names to the group, click the Save button; otherwise, your new buddies will not be added.

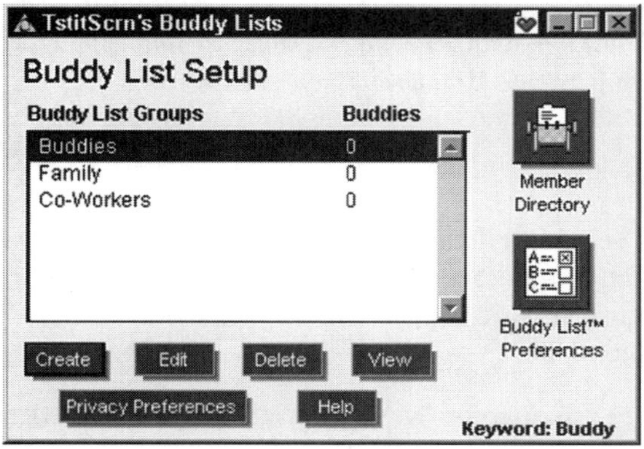

Figure 4-2. The start of your Buddy List.

After you've set up your Buddy List, it can appear automatically every time you sign on to AOL.

Chats and Conferences

Another great way to communicate online is through chat rooms and conferences. The two are similar to one another, but conference rooms but can hold more visitors, and events in conference rooms generally follow protocol: Folks are asked to speak only when called on and don't chat amongst themselves.

Finding a Chat Room

If you want to find a chat room that is organized around a theme or topic, click the People icon on your AOL toolbar, and select Find a Chat, or click Find a Chat on the People Connection main screen. On the left-hand side of the Find a Chat window is a scroll box with about a dozen different categories. At the top of that scroll box, you'll find two tabs. Click the first tab to select from chats created and operated by People Connection. The other tab lists chats created by AOL members like yourself. In both cases, you'll see the same list of categories.

Entering a Chat Room

When you first enter a chat room, you see the chat room window (shown in Figure 4-3). Unless the chat room is empty, you'll begin seeing comments from other people in the room in short order. Each person's comment automatically includes his or her screen name, so everyone knows who said what.

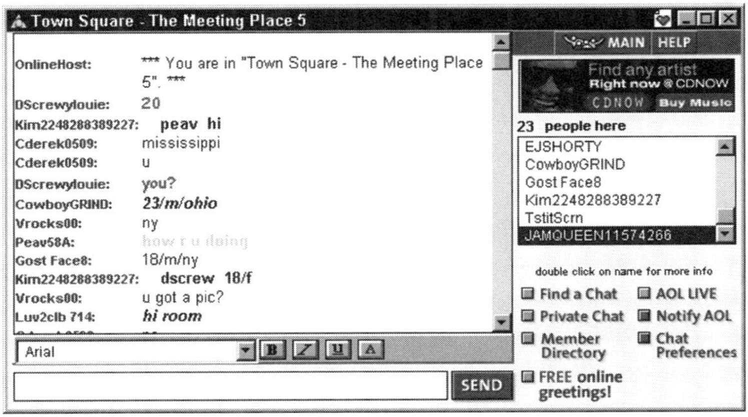

Figure 4-3. A chat room window.

At the very bottom of the chat window is the text box where you type your comments. There's room for about one long sentence in that box. Look at your text, make sure it's what you want to say, and click Send (or press the Enter key). Now you should see your own screen name and comment up in lights!

Who is in the chat room with you? Scroll through the people list on the right-hand side of the window to find out.

About the only thing left to describe are the handy buttons in the lower-right of the chat window:

- **Find a Chat, Private Chat,** and **AOL Live** are there to make moving from chat to chat a bit easier.
- **Member Directory** helps if you're searching for new (and old) friends.
- **Chat Preferences** enables you to change the way you view a chat in your chat window and determine whether you hear chat sounds.
- **Notify AOL** stands at the ready, in case barbarians from the North invade your chat room. If you must notify AOL, be sure to copy the offending chat into the appropriate field in the Notify AOL window.

Message Boards

Message boards are a cornerstone of community on AOL. You'd be hard-pressed to find an online area that lacks a message board. Message boards turn a one-sided presentation of information into a lively give-and-take among people with common interests.

What precisely is a message board? Imagine a large cork bulletin board. Along the top of the corkboard is a row of labels that identify various topics. Perhaps one topic is reserved for official announcements. Beneath each of the other topics people can post written comments, questions, and replies. Instead of a cork board and push pins, you have a computer screen and icons. Better yet, you have all the power and convenience that you normally expect online. Figure 4-4 shows a typical message board.

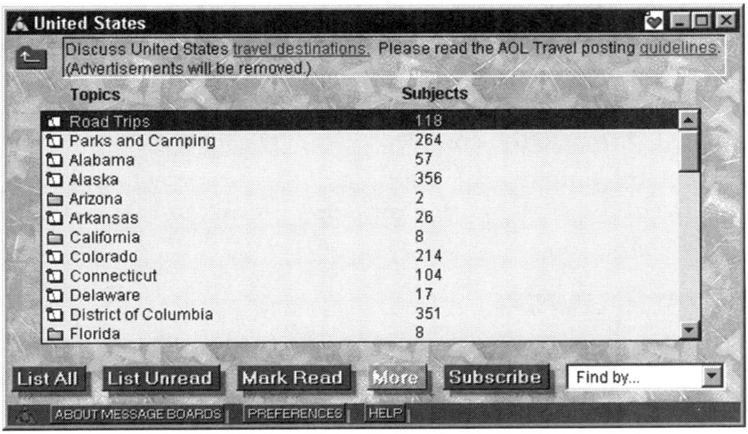

Figure 4-4. A typical message board located at Keyword: **Traveler**.

Finding Communities

Finding communities for message board communications is easy. Pick a forum, any forum! To find the right community (which is a bit harder), it helps to look for one on a topic you're interested in or want to learn more about. Clicking any button or link that suggests a discussion of some sort (like a Chat button) can lead to a message board.

Tip

When you find a message board that you want to call home, add it to your Favorite Places list. You can save an entire message board as a favorite place, or you can save individual topics or messages as favorite places.

Reading Messages

Begin your interaction with your chosen community by reading messages. Reading is easy, and making your way through a message board is only slightly harder. To browse a topic and select messages to read, follow these steps:

1. In the message board window (refer to Figure 4-4), click a topic and then click the List All or List Unread button. Another window opens with that topic in the title bar and lists subjects related to the topic.

2. Double-click a subject to open a window with the subject in the title bar and the first posted message showing in the message box.
3. Use the scroll bar on the side of the message box as needed to read the complete text of the message.
4. Click the buttons at the bottom of the subject window to move through the posted messages for this and other subjects.

Posting Messages

If you want to respond to a message, follow these steps:

1. Go to the topic area of a message board. For example, visit a Member Helping Members message board by using Keyword: **MHM** and clicking the Message Boards link.
2. Double-click a topic that interests you. A window opens with that topic in the title bar.
3. Click Create Subject in the lower-right corner of the topic window to open a Post New Message window.
4. Type a subject in the Subject text box. Every post must have a subject. Be sure that folks reading the subject will understand your question or comment without having to read the post itself.
5. Click in the large text box and type your message.

Tip

When you've finished writing your post, reread it. Be sure you've said what you mean and that it's in line with AOL netiquette, AOL's Terms of Service, and the guidelines for that board.

6. Click the Send button in the lower-right corner of the window. AOL confirms that your message has been sent to the message board by displaying a dialog box — click OK (or press Enter) to dismiss it.

To see the post you've just made, close the message board and reopen it. Your new subject should be there for all to see!

Newsgroups

If you enjoy message boards but hunger for discussions with a wider range of participants, you're ready to step up to newsgroups.

Finding Communities

Speaking of finding things, how do you find newsgroups in the first place? Use Keyword: **Newsgroups**, or choose the Internet icon on the toolbar and select Newsgroups from the drop-down menu.

If you get a message from America Online about selecting the Preferences button, just click OK. You can adjust your preferences later. For now, click the Search All Newsgroups button on the right side of the window and then type your search word(s) into the resulting Search window for a list of newsgroups that match your interest. Double-click any listed newsgroup for a description of the newsgroup and hypertext links that you can use to preview its contents or subscribe to the newsgroup.

Subscribing to Newsgroups

Although a subscription seems like a major commitment, all it really means is that the newsgroups of your choice are added to your personal list of newsgroups, which AOL maintains for you. AOL automatically subscribes you to a handful of useful newsgroups, through which you can learn more about newsgroups and practice your newsgroup skills. Just open the AOL newsgroups area (Keyword: **Newsgroups**) and click the Read My Newsgroups button to view the list.

There are three ways to add newsgroups to that list:

- Click the Search All Newsgroups button to find a newsgroup by topic. Open the newsgroup's description, and click the Subscribe to newsgroup hypertext link.
- Click the Expert Add button when you already know the name of the group you want to join.
- Click the Add Newsgroups button to open a list of newsgroup categories. When you find the newsgroup you want, click the handy Subscribe button.

Reading Messages

Reading newsgroups is very similar to reading message boards, which we describe earlier in this chapter. Begin by opening the Internet Newsgroups window and clicking the Read My Newsgroups button. Your list of subscribed newsgroups appears in alphabetical order.

To open a newsgroup, simply select it and click List Unread or List All. Double-clicking the newsgroup also works (and is the same as clicking List Unread). Reading newsgroups works the same as reading messages on a message board.

Posting Messages

Posting to a newsgroup is also similar to message board posting. The biggest differences aren't technical, but cultural. Each newsgroup has its own culture, social rules, and quirks; we strongly recommend that you get to know a newsgroup by reading it first before you post in it. Read the Newsgroup Etiquette article at the top of the Internet Newsgroups window for a general set of guidelines to follow when posting to newsgroups.

AOL Mail on the Web

AOL Mail on the Web gives you the power to access your e-mail from almost any computer connected to the Internet. All you have to do is access the AOL Mail Web page, sign on with your regular AOL screen name and password, and start reading your e-mail. To sign in to AOL Mail, go to `aolmail.aol.com` or visit the AOL.com home page at `www.aol.com` and click the link for AOL Mail.

Chapter 5

Discovering the Key AOL 5.0 Features

In This Chapter

- Learn about the newest features in AOL 5.0
- Explore You've Got Pictures
- Track your schedule with My Calendar

America Online introduced many new features and improvements in AOL 5.0. In this chapter, we give you a list of those new features, and we take a bit more time to describe two of our favorites: You've Got Pictures and My Calendar.

Looking at What's New in AOL 5.0

As promised, here is a list of the best new features you'll find in AOL 5.0:

- Screen names can be between 3 and 16 characters long.
- Accounts hold up to seven screen names at one time.
- The Welcome screen offers customizable links through the My Places feature (see Chapter 2).
- You've Got Pictures lets you view, organize, and share photos (described in this chapter).
- My Calendar tracks appointments, dates, and personal events (described in this chapter).
- You can set up and use e-mail signatures, which may be automatically added to the bottom of your e-mail messages (see Chapter 3).

- You get access to recently deleted e-mail for up to 24 hours (see Chapter 3).
- You can import/export Favorite Places and Address Books (Windows only).
- Auto AOL sessions work for multiple screen names without disconnecting.
- Get member profiles from Instant Messenger windows.
- Your long filenames are preserved in the Download Manager, libraries, and attached files.
- You can receive enhanced content when accessing AOL via Broadband.
- AOL Search provides improved search capabilities to help you find exactly what you want (see Chapter 7).
- Search directly from the navigation bar. Just type in a search word or words and click the Search button (see Chapter 2).

You've Got Pictures

Are you eager to share your snapshots with family and friends online, but don't have a scanner? Kodak and AOL are changing that with You've Got Pictures, a new service that combines conventional photo processing and online delivery of scanned images.

Bring or mail your film to a participating photo developer (40,000 stores plan to participate) and check off the option for You've Got Pictures. For an extra fee, you get not only the prints you normally receive, but also digital versions of your photos. Within one to three days after the film reaches the lab, you sign on to AOL and hear a familiar voice announcing, "You've got pictures!"

Note If you click the You've Got Pictures icon on the Welcome screen (or use Keyword: **Pictures**) before you receive a roll of developed pictures, upload your own digital photos, or receive a Buddy Album, the Quick Start window (see Figure 5-1) offers a brief introduction to You've Got Pictures.

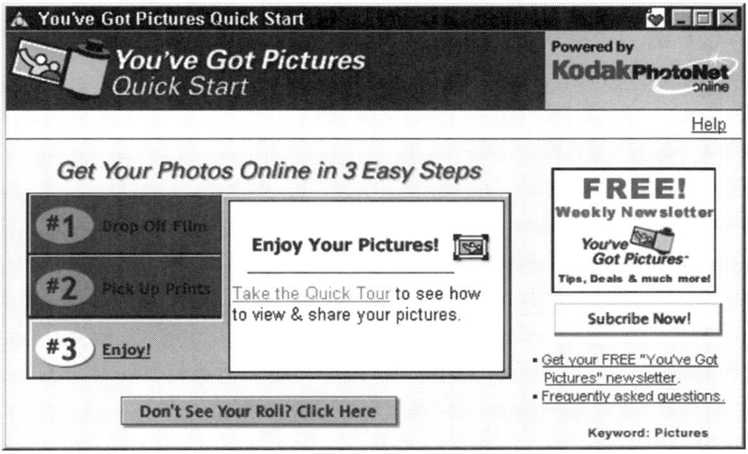

Figure 5-1. Click the Take the Quick Tour link for a slide show about You've Got Pictures.

Whenever you want to view your pictures, go to Keyword: **Pictures**. After you receive your pictures, you can arrange them into online photo albums to be shared with whomever you please, just as long as those folks have Internet access. The following list outlines a few details of the You've Got Pictures service:

- Your newly processed photos are stored online for 30 days, after which they'll be deleted, much like unsaved e-mail. Before they disappear, you can save them online or download them to your hard drive.
- You get free online storage of 50 pictures per screen name (up to 350 images per account, spread among the seven screen names).
- You can rent additional online storage in blocks of 30 images for an additional monthly fee, which will be added to your AOL bill. Storage space can be added in blocks of 30 and decreased by the same amount, too.

The You've Got Pictures window (see Figure 5-2) gives you a choice of four views that you select by clicking the tabs near the top of the window.

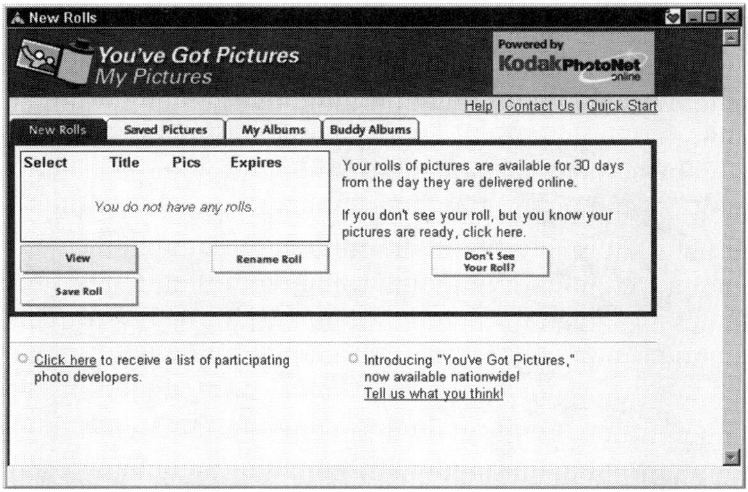

Figure 5-2. Click a tab for access to new rolls, saved pictures, or albums you've created or received.

Here's what these four tabs help you do:

- **New Rolls** gives you access to newly developed rolls of film. When you get a new roll, you can immediately create an album from those pictures and share that album with friends — even if you don't intend to save the pictures yourself. For the first 30 days, you can view all your new pictures by clicking View from the New Rolls tab.
- **Saved Pictures** displays all the pictures you've saved in your online storage area. You can also create an album from the Saved Pictures tab. After an album has been created, you can access it by clicking the My Albums tab, which is also the place to go if you want to share an album with others.
- **My Albums** helps you create albums, gives you access to those albums, and lets you share an album with others. Click the My Albums tab if you want to create a new album incorporating any combination of pictures you've saved and pictures found in your albums and your Buddy Albums (described in this chapter).
- **Buddy Albums** gives you access to albums that you received from others.

Tip

The You've Got Pictures service now offers basic uploading of images that reside on your computer's hard drive provided you have adequate storage available and they adhere to the You've Got Pictures Guidelines. These images and photographs can come from a scanner, CD, or digital camera and must be JPG, JPEG, GIF, or BMP. Simply click the Upload button in your My Albums or Saved Pictures areas and follow the instructions.

Downloading Pictures

Pictures stored online can't be modified. So if you want to edit or manipulate your pictures, you must download them (see Chapter 7 to learn about downloading). Follow these steps to download your pictures:

1. View your pictures under the New Rolls, Saved Pictures, My Albums, or Buddy Albums tab.
2. While viewing your pictures, click the check box next to the picture(s) you want to download.
3. Click Download Pictures at the bottom of the page. You are offered three qualities for the pictures you download.
4. Choose which of the three available qualities you would like for your picture(s) by clicking one of the Download buttons that appear underneath the quality level you prefer.

   Picture qualities are described in terms of use, resolution, download time, and image size. From lowest to highest quality, your options are

   - **E-mail & Web Page Quality:** Downloads quickly and is adequate for casual use online, such as for sharing images with your friends and family.
   - **Print Quality:** Suitable when you want a better version for printing at home.
   - **Premium Offer:** Appeals most to professionals and carries a $1.00 surcharge for each high-quality image downloaded, with a minimum charge of $3.00 per transaction.

Your pictures are downloaded as an executable zip file, with an `.exe` file extension. Select all the various pictures you want to download prior to requesting the download. That way, all the pictures you select are added to the same download file.

After you download the file, you have to "run" it in order to view the picture(s). To do this, open your Windows Start menu, choose Run, click the Browse button, navigate to the folder containing the downloaded file, and click the Open button. A small DOS window opens on-screen to report on the extraction of your pictures. You'll probably want to rename the newly-extracted picture files because You've Got Pictures automatically gives them a filename consisting of an eight-digit number.

Creating an Album

The You've Got Pictures Albums feature is a great way to organize your pictures for your own enjoyment or to share your pictures with friends and relations. Albums are especially convenient because you don't have to download the pictures. The pictures you save online are simply incorporated into a Web page by You've Got Pictures. This makes it easy to share your album with anyone who has Internet access.

To create an album, begin by viewing your pictures. Click the check boxes next to those pictures you'd like to place in an album and click the Create New Album button. Your pictures are displayed in a new window, where you are given a variety of options, including the choice to save your album (see Figure 5-3).

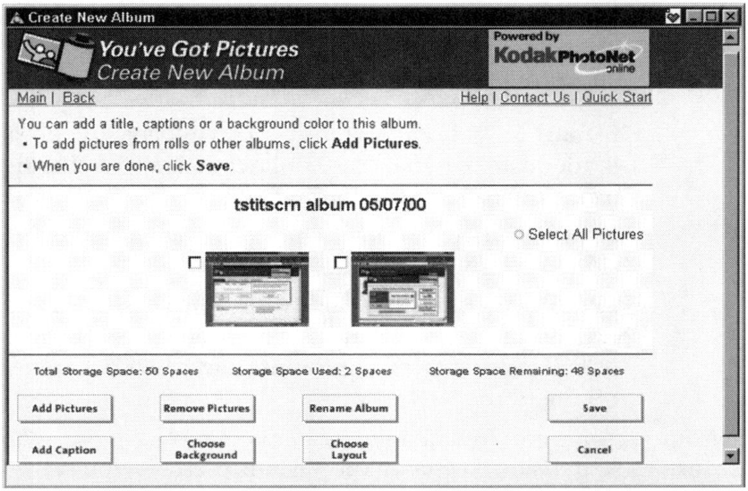

Figure 5-3. Albums of pictures are easy to create.

Albums can contain up to 100 photos. You can add captions for each photo (limited to 32 characters per caption), give each album page a name, add a brief description, and change the background color and the layout of the page. You can also make changes to the album at any time, and everyone who has access to that album will see these changes.

Albums are automatically private, but you can share them with friends and family with AOL accounts or other Internet access. Just add their names to that album's distribution list. They'll receive e-mail telling them how they can view the album, and if they use AOL, they also get the "You've Got Pictures!" message when they sign on.

Note

Those concerned with online safety will be pleased to know that Kids Only (ages 12 and under) and Young Teens (ages 13 to 15) accounts cannot send or receive Buddy Albums or share pictures online.

Anyone receiving a Buddy Album can also order conventional prints and picture CDs, buy gifts such as mugs and T-shirts featuring those images, and save the album to his or her own Saved Pictures space. This means that grandma and grandpa can cover their coffee table with framed enlargements without needing the original negatives. (This also means you shouldn't share any photos that you wouldn't want the world to see.)

Definition

AOL has instituted a set of You've Got Pictures guidelines that apply the Terms of Service to the unique issues faced by You've Got Pictures. The guidelines address issues such as illegal images, copyright infringement, solicitation of business, and the like. If you need additional help with You've Got Pictures, try Keyword: **Picture Help** for plenty of instructions, tips, and answers to frequently asked questions.

Using My Calendar

So much to do, so little time! Now that you've added AOL to your social life, how can you keep track of all the online chats, meetings, TV shows, play dates, ball games, and cultural events that fill your days (and nights)? Take advantage of the latest addition to AOL's lineup of cool features, My Calendar.

To get started with My Calendar, just click the My Calendar icon on either the AOL Welcome screen or the AOL toolbar, or use Keyword: **Calendar**. As a first-time visitor, you'll be asked to supply your time zone, zip code (so My Calendar can suggest events happening in your area), and birth date (if you want a daily horoscope). If you wish, AOL will add 5-day weather forecasts, too. You can always change any of these settings by clicking the Options button at the bottom of the main calendar window (see Figure 5-4).

My Calendar is a good bit more than an old-fashioned appointment book. Thanks to its online connections, every appointment you set up can be shared with anyone you please, via e-mail. My Calendar also includes an Idea List and Event Calendar that list online chats, TV programs, movies, sports, and cultural events that you can add to your calendar with just a click or two of your mouse. You should also keep your eyes open for the My Calendar icon wherever you travel on AOL and the World Wide Web. If you see it, click it to add that item to your calendar.

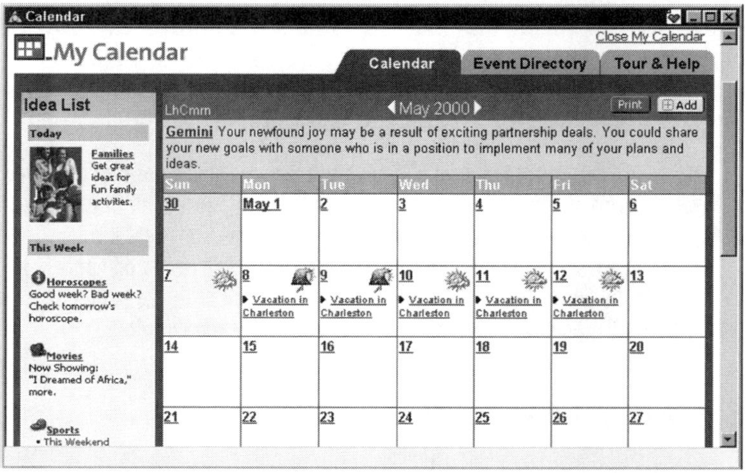

Figure 5-4. My Calendar opens with a monthly overview of your schedule.

Customize your calendar by selecting a one-day or one-week calendar view, and add local weather forecasts, your daily horoscope, and your choice of national and religious holidays. Once you get started with My Calendar, you'll be amazed by just how much you can do with it.

Chapter 6

Organizing and Customizing AOL

In This Chapter

- Customize your software with preferences
- Keep information within reach with Favorite Places
- Discover how to get the current news and weather
- Track your investments with online portfolios

The AOL experience gets richer with every passing year, and the list of options grows right along with it. You can customize your e-mail, chat rooms, downloads, Personal Filing Cabinet, the AOL toolbar, and your Buddy List. The privacy-minded can protect themselves and their families with features such as Parental Controls and Privacy Preferences. We hope this introduction to organizing and customizing helps you discover and adjust all these settings to your taste.

Setting Preferences

You gain access to most preferences by clicking the My AOL icon on the AOL toolbar and then selecting Preferences from the drop-down menu. Figure 6-1 shows the Preferences window that appears.

Use the following steps to set preferences in the Preferences window:

1. Click the icon for the preferences that you want to customize. A dialog box then appears. Figure 6-2 shows the dialog box that you see when you click the General icon.
2. Click the option buttons and/or check boxes to set the associated features on or off.

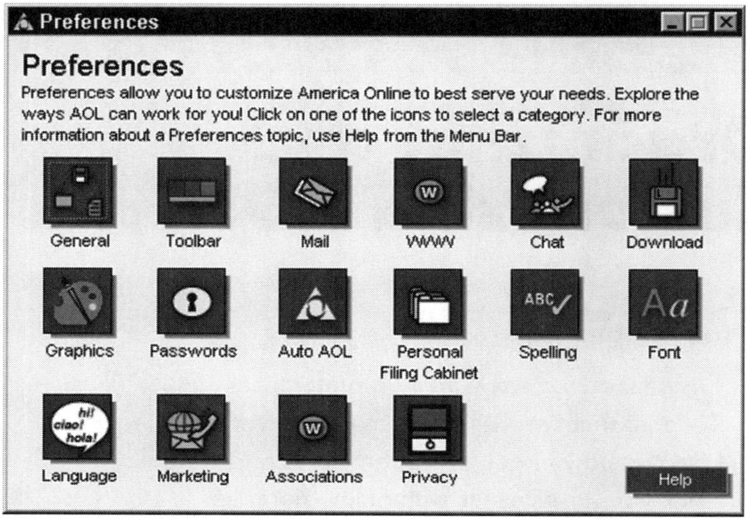

Figure 6-1. Your preferences are always within reach under the My AOL icon on the toolbar.

3. When you're finished setting your preferences, click OK to save your settings or click Cancel to close this window without saving your settings.

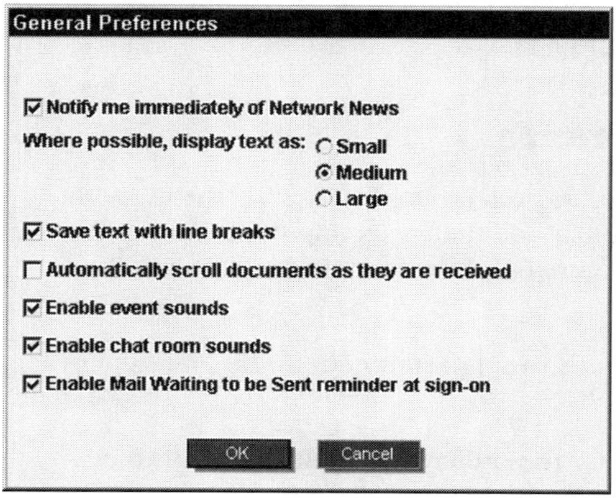

Figure 6-2. General Preferences settings control text formats and sounds, among other things.

We've also gathered information on other important options and settings as well as help you find them. In this chapter, we discuss the most important or useful of these preferences in the order they appear in the Preferences window.

General Preferences encompass a collection of announcement, text, and sound preference settings, the most important of which are listed in the following table.

Preference	Its Purpose	Default Setting
Save text with line breaks	Automatically inserts a hard return at the end of every line of text for any e-mail.	On
Enable event sounds	Turn on or off sounds such as "You've got mail!," "Welcome," "Goodbye," and the Instant Message chime.	On
Enable chat room sounds	Play sounds in a chat room so that others who have the same sound file installed on their hard disks can hear the sound.	On

Toolbar Preferences affect the toolbar at the top of the AOL screen, which can be customized to your needs. You can make changes to how and where the toolbar appears and make other adjustments listed in this table.

Preference	Its Purpose	Default Setting
Navigation	Use Previous and Next navigation arrows to track open windows only.	Off
History Trail	Clear the History Trail after each Sign Off or Switch Screen Name	Off

Tip: The History Trail remembers the online areas and Web pages you've visited so you can return again, even if you signed off in the interim. If you share your computer with other members of the family, you may prefer to have AOL erase the trail every time someone signs off.

Mail Preferences provide greater control over mail you read, send, and save in your Personal Filing Cabinet. The following table highlights some of these settings.

Preference	Its Purpose	Default Setting
Retain all mail I send in my Personal Filing Cabinet	Saves a copy of all e-mail you send on your hard disk.	Off
Retain all mail I read in my Personal Filing Cabinet	Saves a copy of all e-mail you read on your hard disk.	Off
Perform a spell check before sending mail	Automatically initiates a spell check when you click the Send button to deliver an e-mail.	Off
Use AOL style quoting/ Use Internet style quoting	Toggles between AOL-style quoting (quoted text surrounded with <<double brackets>>) and Internet-style quoting (quoted text preceded with a single > bracket).	AOL-style quoting
Keep my old mail online <number> days after I read it	The number of days (from 3 to 7) before automatic deletion of your e-mail.	3 days

Web Preferences are a complex set of tools, just as your Web browser is a complex bit of software. These preferences affect your built-in AOL browser (Microsoft Internet Explorer). If you're using a separate browser (such as Netscape Navigator), you'll have to open your browser to find its preference settings. Web Preferences are divided into four sections: General, Security, Content, and Web Graphics. Click the tabs at the top of the screen to switch between these sections. We describe some of the preferences from the General tab here:

- **Home page:** Determines which page opens when you click the Home Page icon on the AOL toolbar. Type in the URL of the page you find most useful. The Use Default button restores AOL.com (`www.aol.com`) as your home page.
- **Temporary Internet files:** Your browser automatically saves Web pages and other Web files on your hard disk. This means you can access them again, offline, and it also speeds access of those pages if you revisit them online. This can use a lot of disk space (which may hurt your computer's performance), but you can clear out that disk space. Click Delete Files to open a dialog box in which you can delete all files in the Temporary Internet Files folder.

Chat Preferences affect features of chat rooms, private rooms, conference rooms, and auditoriums on AOL. They can be accessed by clicking the Preferences button in the chat room or by visiting the Preferences area of My AOL. The most common choices appear in the following table.

Preference	Its Purpose	Default Setting
Notify me when members arrive	Triggers the Online Host to announce that a member has entered the chat room	Off
Notify me when members leave	Triggers the Online Host to announce that a member has left the chat room	Off
Enable chat room sounds	Allows people in chat rooms to play sounds so that others who have the same sound file installed on their hard disks can hear the sound	On

Download Preferences affect files you download from AOL's file libraries and forums, and attached e-mail files.

Preference	Its Purpose	Default Setting
Display image files on download	Enables AOL to begin displaying image files (in GIF, JPG, BMP, or ART formats) while they're downloading	On
Automatically decompress files at sign-off	Automatically decompresses files in ZIP format (Windows) or Stuffit format (Mac) when you sign off from AOL	On
Delete ZIP files after decompression	Deletes the original compressed format (such as the ZIP format) after a file has been decompressed	Off
Use this directory as default for downloads	Allows you to specify the folder to use for downloaded files	`C:\America Online5.0\download`

Graphics Preferences control a variety of features relating to downloading and displaying images and adding pictures to e-mail. AOL also speeds your online experience by saving many graphics, icons, buttons, and other on-screen images on your hard disk so they don't have to be retransmitted by AOL over slow telephone lines. Although this is similar to how temporary Internet files work, this particular function only relates to graphics used by AOL and its forums, not the Web.

- **Maximum disk space to use for online art: <number> megabyte(s):** As you visit more areas on AOL, you will accumulate more artwork on your hard drive. This setting limits the amount of space AOL can use (so as not to fill your hard drive) and allows your computer to reach a balance between speed and available hard drive space. (Default setting: 20 megabytes.)
- **Notify before opening mail containing pictures:** This safety warning reminds people that an image contained in an e-mail message may turn out to be an objectionable one. If you don't need this warning, you can disable it here. (Default setting: On.)

Password Preferences let you bypass your password when you sign on or add a password to your Personal Filing Cabinet so that it's more secure. It's unlikely that you'll use both of these options at the same time, since one reduces security and the other enhances it.

- **Password:** If you plan to use the Sign-On option, this must be the password you use to sign on to AOL. If you plan to only use the PFC option, you can use any password you please. (Default setting: blank.)
- **Sign-On:** Eliminates the need to enter your password before you sign on to AOL. This reduces the security of your account. (Default setting: Off.)
- **PFC:** Adds password protection to your PFC. When this option is on, your PFC cannot be accessed without entering the password, whether or not you are signed on. (Default setting: Off.)

Automatic AOL can send and retrieve your e-mail, file downloads, and message board postings while you're asleep or even out of the country.

Personal Filing Cabinet Preferences: Your Personal Filing Cabinet can take up a lot of hard disk space, so AOL provides settings in the Personal Filing Cabinet Preferences window that limit and manage the hard disk space occupied by your PFC files.

Spelling Preferences: Spelling preference settings give you control over which rules will and will not be enforced, and give you access to your personal spelling dictionary.

Font Preferences: You can make all your e-mail, chat, and Instant Messages distinctive by changing your font preference settings. These settings apply to every e-mail, chat, and Instant Message used on your account, regardless of screen name, so there's room for family disagreements.

Language Preferences: America Online is available worldwide, and some of AOL's online content is available in more than one language. Select a language (or languages) from the Available Languages list and click the Add button to state which languages you can choose from when AOL offers you a choice.

Marketing Preferences: AOL is the world's largest online shopping destination and uses many different methods to reach its membership with product and service offers. AOL doesn't want to alienate you with undesired offers or make you feel like your privacy has been breached, so it offers Marketing Preferences to give you a choice in these matters. You must be signed on to AOL to set your Marketing Preferences.

Association Preferences: The Windows desktop can have icons for browsing the Web, sending e-mail, and reading newsgroups. This preference allows you to designate AOL as the application you want to use when you click those icons on the Windows desktop. You can also access some of these settings from the Windows Control Panel.

Privacy Preferences relate to Buddy Lists and Instant Messages, and can be accessed either in the Buddy List setup window or on the Preferences screen. You can create a single list of screen names, which can be used in one of the following ways.

Under Choose Your Privacy Preferences, select one of these options:

- **Allow all AOL members and AOL Instant Messenger users:** Anyone on AOL (or using AOL Instant Messenger via the Internet) can view you on his or her Buddy List and send you an Instant Message. (This is the default.)
- **Block AOL Instant Messenger users only:** AOL members have full Buddy List and/or Instant Message access, but Instant Messenger users (Internet users) do not.
- **Block only those people whose screen names I list:** Create a list of the people you never want to hear from, and/or banish yourself from their Buddy Lists. Anyone else can still access you.
- **Allow only those people whose screen names I list:** This provides a high level of personal privacy, as only those you place on your list may send you Instant Messages and/or see you on their Buddy Lists.
- **Block all AOL members and AOL Instant Messenger users:** This is the maximum privacy setting. Nobody can see you on his or her Buddy List, and/or send you an Instant Message.

Under Apply Preferences to the Following Features, you can apply the preceding privacy preferences only to Buddy Lists, or to both Buddy Lists and Instant Messages, as follows:

- **Buddy List:** People you have blocked can't see you on their Buddy Lists, but they can still send you Instant Messages.
- **Buddy List and Instant Message:** You won't be seen on Buddy Lists or receive Instant Messages from those whom you have blocked.

Setting Other Preferences

You can modify **Billing and Account** information by using Keyword: **Billing** or by choosing Member Services Online Help from the Help menu and clicking the My Account button in the resulting AOL Help window.

To access your **Buddy List Preferences,** click the Setup button on the Buddy List window (Keyword: **BuddyView**) and click Buddy List Preferences in the resulting Buddy List Setup window.

Message Boards and **Newsgroups** also have their own preferences, which you can access from the Message Board and Newsgroup windows.

Finding Your Favorite Places

The Favorite Places feature can make getting to where you want to go even faster. Each one of your screen names has its own Favorite Places list, which appears when you click the Favorites icon on the toolbar. After you add a favorite place to your list, all you have to do is click the Favorites icon, select the place from the list, and you're on your way.

AOL lets you create a favorite place for nearly any window you can open on AOL, including any place on the Web. Navigate to the place you want to add to the list, and look for the little red-and-white heart icon on the right-hand side of the window's title bar.

Note

Your Favorite Places list can become long and unruly. If it becomes too long, "More Favorites" will appear at the bottom of your list. But don't worry! You can bring order to the chaos by adding new Favorite Places folders, rearranging the places in your list, deleting unwanted items, and otherwise organizing your Favorite Places.

Follow these steps to reorganize items in your Favorite Places list:

1. Click the Favorite icon and choose Favorite Places to open an editable version of your Favorite Places list, as shown in Figure 6-3.

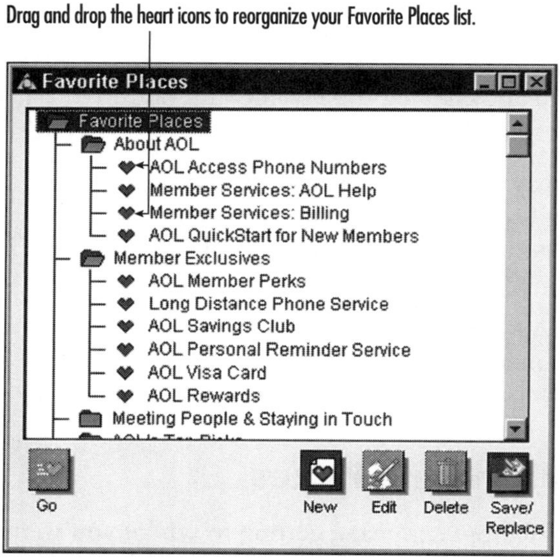

Figure 6-3. The editable Favorite Places list.

2. Click the New button to create a new subcategory folder, which appears as a submenu on your Favorites menu.
3. Drag and drop the heart icons from existing items in your list to place them into your new folder.
4. Use the Delete, Edit, and New buttons at the bottom of the window to delete unwanted items, edit the titles (or URLs) of existing favorite places or folders, and even create new favorite places if you happen to know the URL of the Web page.

5. Click the X in the upper-right corner of the Favorite Places window when you're finished organizing your list.

Getting the News

AOL will send you the news you need, automatically. AOL News Profiles is your own private clipping service. Create a profile outlining your interests, and AOL will send you e-mail containing stories from a wide variety of news organizations whenever that news becomes available. All you have to do to get started is go to Keyword: **News Profiles,** click Create Your News Profiles, and fill in the forms.

Tracking Investments

Along similar lines, stock market watchers will appreciate Keyword: **Portfolio Direct,** which will e-mail you a daily report containing news on up to 20 stocks of your choice. And whether you're an active investor or an armchair capitalist, AOL makes it simple to track your investments and test investment strategies at Keyword: **My Portfolios.** Every screen name on an AOL account can maintain up to 20 online portfolios, each of which can contain up to 100 stocks, mutual funds, money market funds, and financial indices.

Chapter 7

Exploring AOL and the Internet

In This Chapter

- Search for information on AOL and the Web
- Find family and friends online
- Discover valuable files and download them to your computer

In the hunt for great information, picture AOL as a whopping, big-city main branch library. The librarians maintain numerous indexes and catalogs, and many methods of searching those catalogs for just the information you need. When you know how to use all these search methods, the information you seek tumbles onto your computer screen.

Now, if that's America Online, just imagine the Internet, an international network that connects you to countless information resources — venerable universities and museums, governments big and small, corporations, foundations, clubs, non-profit organizations, and passionate, amateur hobbyists. Although nearly all these millions of resources have local indexes, no single organization offers a master catalog of the Internet. In fact, the task is so huge and the information lying beyond so valuable, that indexing, cataloging, and searching the Internet has become a multibillion-dollar industry.

AOL Search Tools

AOL provides users with a variety of tools for searching both within AOL and on the World Wide Web.

AOL Search

AOL Search does something no other search tool can do: It searches both AOL and the Web in one easy step. You can reach AOL Search one of three ways:

- Click the Search button on the AOL toolbar.
- Choose AOL Search from the Favorites icon on the AOL toolbar.
- Use the Keyword: **Search**.

Here are our best tips and techniques to help you craft good search words and phrases:

- Be specific. If you're looking for information about your new dog, type the dog's breed such as **Alaskan Malamute** rather than simply **dog**. If you're looking for an exact phrase (such as dog bark), put quotes around it.
- Use boolean operators, which is just a fancy way to say, "Use AND, OR, and NOT in your searches." Including these words limits your search and generally produces better results. For example, type **malamute or husky** to find all articles matching either breed of sled dog, but not both.
- Don't worry about case. Capitalization rarely matters.
- Don't worry about suffixes. Most search engines will treat the words *bark, barks, barked,* and *barking* as the same word.

Once you've decided on a search word or phrase that best describes what you are seeking, enter it into the entry field at the top of the AOL Search window and click the Search button (see Figure 7-1).

AOL Search opens a new window, shown in Figure 7-2, in which it displays the search results. In the main section of the window are the main matching categories, followed by the matching sites. Matching sites link you directly to areas or forums that usually contain information and/or articles with information matching your word or phrase. The matching sites are displayed in order of relevancy. (The percentage indicates how closely a page matches your word or phrase.)

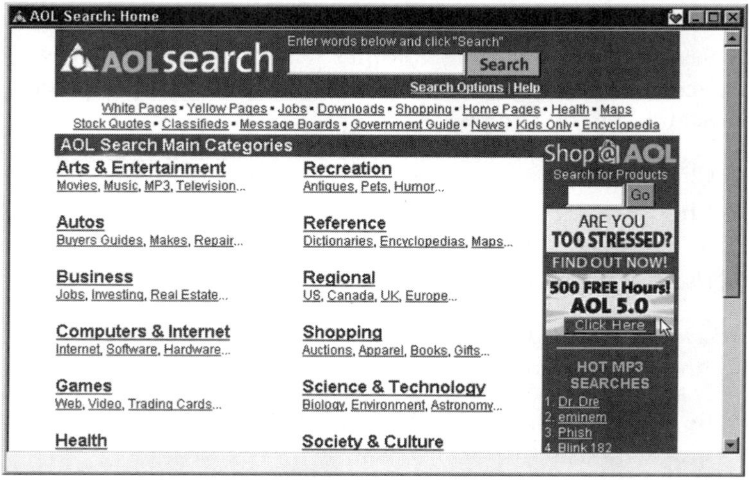

Figure 7-1. AOL Search stands ready to search for you.

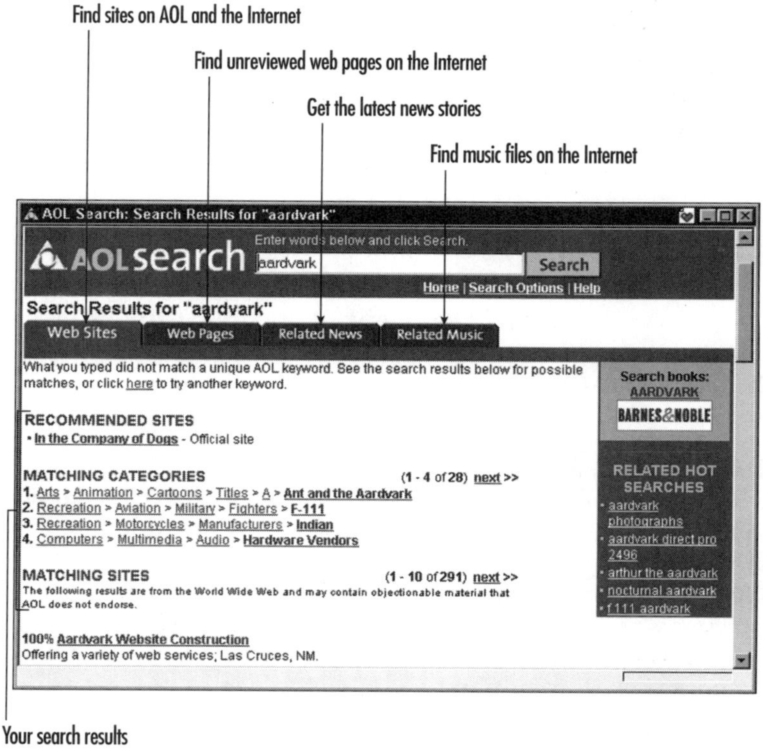

Figure 7-2. AOL displays your keyword search results.

Note: If AOL Search finds entire categories that match your search word or phrase, it displays the results near the top of the window. Click one of these categories to see a list of sites, which may or may not offer what you need.

Channel Searches

Another way to search for content on America Online is to go to the source. In this case, that means searching on the channel level. For example, you may know that gymnastics would be somewhere in the Sports Channel, so a channel search would likely be fruitful.

Follow these steps to do a channel search:

1. Go to a channel via keyword. (All channel names are also keywords.) If you're not sure which channel you need, use one of these options:
   - The buttons on the left-hand side of the Welcome screen (or the main screen for any channel).
   - The Channels icon on the toolbar.
   - Keyword: **Channels.**
2. Once the channel of choice is open on your screen, look for an option called Search & Explore or simply Search (it is usually near the bottom of the channel window). Alternatively, use Keyword: **Channel Guide**, choose a channel, and look for the Search option.
3. Click the channel's Search option to open it. A channel's search and explore window generally offers an A-Z guide of all forums in the channel, as well as links to popular or helpful features.

   If you don't find what you seek in the text, click the Search button below it to open the channel's dedicated search page.

To use a channel search page, follow these steps:

1. Type your search word or phrase into the top field. You could click the Start Searching button now, but it pays to spend a few extra minutes refining your search.

2. You can select the type of results you're seeking (for example, all articles or only those that are new in the last 24 hours).
3. When you're ready, click the Start Searching button (or just press the Enter key). The results are displayed in the same window.

Local Searches

You often get more detailed, specific results with a local search on the forum level. The downside is that you're only searching one forum's content and thus won't find anything that isn't available in the forum.

To perform a local search, go directly to the forum in question by using its keyword. Alternatively, use Keyword: **Channel Guide** (see Figure 7-3) to browse the forums available in each channel and then choose one.

Note: Finding a search option in a forum is more hit-or-miss than in a channel — not every forum can be searched. If you see a Search or a Find link, click it. Otherwise, your best bet is to look for a Help or a Site Map link.

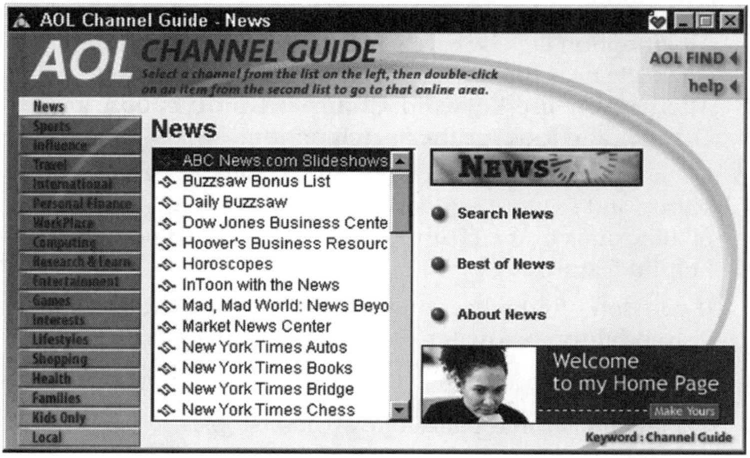

Figure 7-3. Channel Guide can be your virtual compass.

Keyword Search

Keywords are another useful tool for finding information on America Online. Although you may mostly use keywords to reach familiar areas, you can also use them to explore new areas. One way you can do this is to simply guess a keyword, which works even if your guess isn't an actual keyword. If your guess doesn't work, follow these steps:

1. Type in a keyword the way you would type in a search word. (Use the text box on the navigation bar, or press Ctrl+K on Windows or +K on the Mac.) Use general search words rather than specific ones.

> **Tip** AOL automatically initiates a search for your word or phrase on AOL and the Internet. Any results are displayed in a new window. If no alternate keywords are suggested, AOL offers the opportunity to search on your word.

2. If you get an alternate keyword that looks promising, select it in the list.
3. Click Open (or press Enter).

AOL Hometown

AOL Hometown is a free service that lets you build your own home page on the Internet. You can include information, photos, and links to other places on the Internet. Once your home page is built, you can include it in AOL Hometown and share it with the world. To get started with AOL Hometown, use Keyword: **Hometown**.

Using the Member Directory and Other People Finders

AOL and the Internet are great places to find information. And what better information can you find than the e-mail address of a long-lost friend or relative? Your search can start right in AOL's own Member Directory and spread outward from there.

Member Directory

Everyone on AOL who has a member profile is listed in the Member Directory, and it's completely searchable. To do a quick search of the Member Directory, follow these steps:

1. Open the Member Directory — choose Search AOL Member Directory from the People icon on the toolbar or use Keyword: **Members**.
2. Type in a search word or phrase in the first field of the resulting window. Alternatively, you can type a name (first, last, or both) in the Member Name field and/or a location (city, state, country, and so on) in the Location field to refine your search.
3. Click Search (or press Enter) to begin your search. AOL displays the Member Directory search results in a new window.
4. Double-click a screen name to view the complete member profile.

The results window lists the first 20 profiles that match your search word or phrase. The results aren't listed in any logical order, so you may need to browse through them to find what you're seeking.

E-mail Finder

The AOL Member Directory is a powerful tool for finding people on AOL, but what about people who aren't on AOL? The AOL E-mail Finder can help you locate virtually anyone with an e-mail address, whether they're on AOL or not. Use Keyword: **Email Finder** to go directly to the Web-based search page.

White Pages

Not everyone has an e-mail address yet. AOL recognizes this and makes an international, fully searchable White Pages available. In addition to phone numbers, the AOL White Pages offers e-mail addresses, street mailing addresses, neighborhood maps, driving directions, lists of nearby businesses, and more. You can reach the AOL White Pages one of two ways: by using the Keyword: **White Pages** or by choosing White Pages from the Internet icon on the toolbar.

Locating Places and Things

When you need to find a business, its address, and its phone number, where better to turn than the phone book? Here's a better idea: Use the electronic version of the yellow pages and white pages on AOL!

Yellow Pages

An AOL Yellow Pages listing includes a map, driving instructions, and (sometimes) fax numbers and e-mail addresses! AOL's Yellow Pages is part of AOL Search and AOL Find. It can be reached one of two ways: by using Keyword: **Yellow Pages** or by choosing Yellow Pages from the Internet icon on the toolbar.

You can search for businesses by either business category or business name, and you must narrow the search by selecting which state to search. If you know which city to search, so much the better! Category searches are most accurate if you select a category from the Yellow Pages' Category list.

Search Engines

Search results are scored, so Web sites that seem to most closely fit your needs will be at the top of the resulting list. This doesn't mean that what the computer "thinks" are the best sites for your needs are actually the ones that suit you best. As we've noted, a search is only as good as your search word or phrase, and the nature of a search can bury you in useless Web sites while the best information lies tantalizingly out of reach.

Definition

Search engines are the detectives of the Internet. Using automated programs called bots and spiders, search engines probe the contents of every Web site they can find. Visitors to a search engine (such as AOL Search, which we've already discussed), type in a search word or phrase, and initiate a search. The search program (or *engine*) goes to work, combing its files for every Web site that even remotely matches the search phrase.

The companies in the search engine business (and it is a business) know this all too well, and take pains to make their search results as useful as they can possibly be. Many include convenient features such as a More Like This link so that when you do find a perfect match, the search engine can find more of a good thing.

Find It Online

Many search engines are available, but several popular ones are AltaVista (`www.altavista.com`), the Go Network (`www.go.com`), and Google (`www.google.com`).

Finding Files

AOL is truly a goldmine of free and low-cost treasures. The newly acquainted often overlook it, or worse yet, don't realize it even exists. We have the treasure map to the goodies, and we'll show you the way. Before we embark on our quest, let's get a handle on two important concepts: files and downloading.

Files are information stored on a computer or transported between computers. A word processing document is a file, and so is a picture viewed on a computer screen. Of course, some files are games, utilities, and business applications.

Downloading is the process of transferring a file from AOL to your own computer. The Computing Channel has prepared an entire area to teach you how to download called, appropriately enough, How to Download. You can find it quickly at Keyword: **How to Download**.

The Download Center is AOL's central treasure chamber. Here you'll find thousands of files, including vibrant graphics, rich sounds, and valuable programs that can make you as powerful as a genie or as rich as King Midas (well, almost). You don't need a magic lamp to find this treasure, either. Where can you find files to download? Go to Keyword: **Download Center**.

Viruses and Trojan Horses

Along with the benefits of downloading files, we must also accept the risks involved — namely, contracting viruses or encountering Trojan Horses.

Definition

Viruses are specific kinds of files designed by their programmers to cause damage. Viruses generally damage the files on your computer's hard drive. *Trojan Horses,* on the other hand, are dangerous files disguised as useful or desirable programs. Trojan Horses generally contain objectionable or inappropriate images, conceal viruses, or even compromise your AOL account or credit card information.

Your best defense against viruses and Trojan Horses is knowledge. For this, we direct you to the Anti-Virus Center at Keyword: **Virus**. Here you find plenty of information about what is a virus, a Trojan Horse, or just a hoax. You can also download demo versions of anti-virus programs or purchase commercial software.

FTP (File Transfer Protocol)

Definition

FTP, or File Transfer Protocol, is a system used to transfer entire files across the Internet. FTP is a much more efficient and reliable way to exchange files than e-mail, but not everyone has the software needed to use it.

Luckily for you, FTP is built into your AOL software. In fact, downloading files from FTP is very much like downloading files from an AOL file library. Follow these steps to use FTP:

1. Click the Internet icon on the AOL toolbar.
2. Select FTP from the drop-down menu or use Keyword: **FTP**.
3. Browse the Best of FTP folder in the main window and open one of the recommended FTP sites. Alternatively, you can click the Go To FTP button on the right side of the window and choose one of the favorite sites listed there.
4. If you prefer to go directly to another site for which you have the address, click the Other Site button at the bottom of the window and type in the requested information.

Many companies and organizations maintain FTP sites, although you may need a username and password to gain access. Other FTP sites may be accessed by anyone. AOL supplies a list of useful public FTP sites you can visit, but you're also free to search for and visit other sites.

Chapter 8

Shopping Online

In This Chapter

- Staying safe with the AOL Shopping Guarantee
- Speeding up your shopping with AOL Quick Checkout
- Using Customer Service
- Shopping from the world through the classifieds

If you enjoy mail-order catalogs, shopping online should come as second nature to you. You're free to browse, and browse, and browse at any time of the day or night, with no salespeople to pressure or intimidate you. Price comparisons are easy, because you can open windows into as many stores as you like at the same time.

Although you'll find shopping opportunities in many of AOL's channels and forums, AOL's Shopping Channel (also known as Shop@AOL and shown in Figure 8-1) is the best place to start. Click the Shopping button on the left side of your Welcome screen or use the Keyword: **Shopping**.

An Overview of Shopping Online Safely

Did you know that shopping on AOL is statistically safer than shopping at your local mall? AOL hasn't received even one report of a compromised credit card since the Shopping Channel opened its doors in 1996. How does AOL do it? AOL provides a secure environment for credit card transactions by encrypting all data sent and received during the purchase. This means that even if someone intercepted the transmission (very, very unlikely, but still a remote possibility), that person wouldn't be able to make heads or tails of the information.

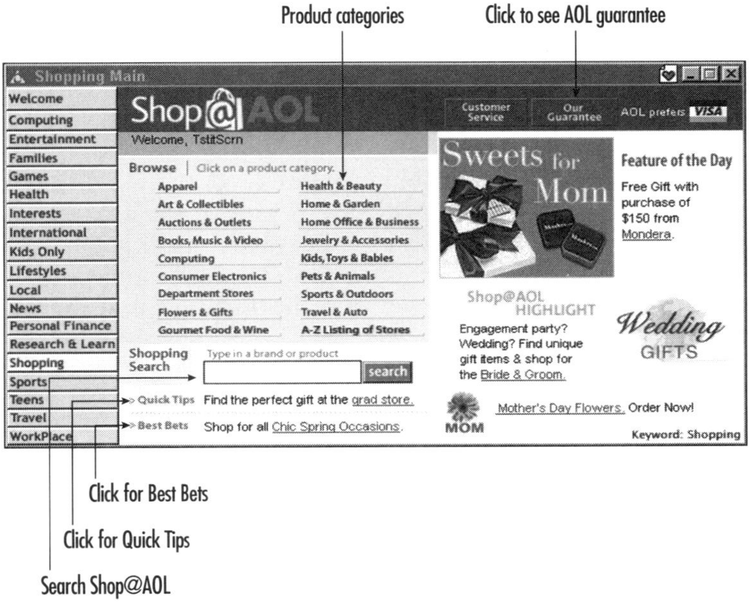

Figure 8-1. Shop@AOL is an electronic bazaar of goods and services.

AOL guarantees this secure environment only with its certified merchants, however; so your safety is also your responsibility. Be careful not to give your credit card information or any other personal information to an unauthorized party. If you receive an unsolicited e-mail or Instant Message requesting your credit card information, you can be pretty sure the message is fraudulent.

Note The only times you will be asked for your credit card number are during the initial AOL registration and when making a purchase online. If you receive what you believe is a fraudulent credit card request, notify AOL immediately at Keyword: **TOS**. You can also send e-mail to screen name MarketMail.

AOL Customer Service and Shopping Guarantee

AOL goes out of its way to be sure you have a happy AOL shopping experience. If you have a problem with a merchant, your first stop should be its own customer service department. AOL's Certified Merchants Program requires merchants to provide a high level of customer service, so most problems should be resolved without AOL's help. If you can't work things out with the merchant, though, AOL is ready to back you up.

AOL's customer service representatives are on duty from 8 a.m. to 2 a.m. Eastern time to help with any of your shopping questions or problems. Customer Service is easy to find; all you have to do is click the Customer Service button on the Shopping Channel's main screen, or use Keyword: **Shopping Customer Service**.

If you have a problem with a merchant, the more information you have for AOL's customer service representatives, the better. Be prepared with a written description containing these things:

- Name of the merchant
- Date of purchase
- Price you paid
- What you've done to resolve the problem and how the merchant responded

AOL carefully selects, evaluates, and tests merchants before they sell merchandise on AOL. All merchants must meet or exceed a certain level of service. That includes

- Processing orders promptly
- Conducting transactions securely
- Shipping the product professionally
- Responding to customer questions quickly
- Adopting policies to ensure customer privacy

Those merchants that meet these standards become certified and are entitled to display the AOL Certified Merchant Guarantee seal of approval (see Figure 8-2).

Now what about this guarantee? AOL backs up every purchase made through its Certified Merchants Program. Here's how it works: If you have a problem with a merchant, first contact the merchant in question. Should the merchant refuse to provide a satisfactory resolution, you can contact AOL to intervene on your behalf. If the merchant still does not comply with its return policy, AOL will refund the full purchase price.

Note Remember to read each merchant's return policy before you make purchases; not all merchants will refund purchase prices if you have a problem. You can usually find refund policies in a merchant's customer service area.

Figure 8-2. Notice the Certified Merchant Guarantee seal at the lower right of the merchant's window.

AOL Quick Checkout

Welcome to the express checkout lane! With a little help from AOL Quick Checkout, you can fly through the online stores in record time. Sign up for Quick Checkout one of two ways:

- Visit Keyword: **Quick Checkout** (see Figure 8-3).
- Click Set Up Quick Checkout Now when you check out the normal way at any merchant who accepts Quick Checkout.

AOL Quick Checkout saves you some of the time and trouble of entering your credit card and shipping information every time you make a purchase and helps you avoid typing errors. It saves information on up to 10 of your credit/debit cards and the shipping addresses of up to 50 of your friends and relatives on AOL's carefully secured computers.

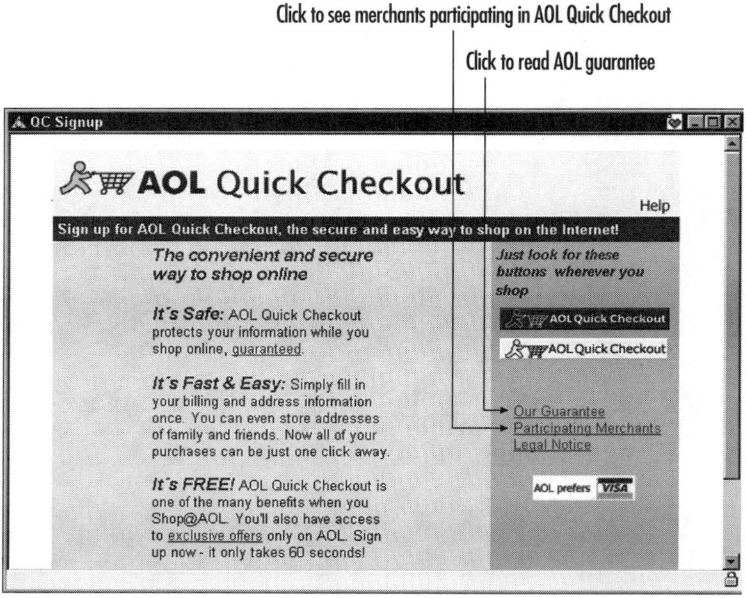

Figure 8-3. Quick Checkout, where the express lane is always open.

Whenever you reach the checkout at a participating AOL merchant, Quick Checkout will automatically supply your default information (your preferred credit card and regular shipping address). If you want to use a different card or ship the goods to someone else listed in your Quick Checkout address book, just click Edit and make the desired changes. Of course, you can also replace the information supplied by Quick Checkout — just type in something completely different.

Tip: Quick Checkout is also the place to go if you want to add, delete, or modify credit card and address information, or to get in-depth information on how Quick Checkout works. There's also a special Quick Checkout Customer Service number at 877-385-2330 if you have problems or questions regarding your Quick Checkout account.

There's a lot of trust involved in any relationship in which you provide such sensitive financial information, and AOL goes to great lengths to earn that trust:

- Your Quick Checkout account is protected by a separate password. The first time you use Quick Checkout during an online session you'll be asked for that password.
- To make changes to your Quick Checkout information, you are also asked a security question, the answer for which you provide when you set up your Quick Checkout account.
- Your information is protected from prying eyes. Once it has been entered into the system, your credit card number will not be displayed on-screen. Only the last four digits of your card number will be shown so you can recognize the card.
- Your information is stored at AOL on computers that are not accessible via the Internet.
- The highest level of SSL encryption available with your browser protects credit card information as it flows between your computer and AOL (128 bit with Internet Explorer 5.0, which is the browser supplied with AOL 5.0).
- Only screen names with Parental Controls set to 18+ can create Quick Checkout accounts.
- You are free to delete information or your account at any time, and AOL erases that information immediately.

Of course, computer security becomes even more important once you set up a Quick Checkout account. Be sure your passwords are unique, hard to guess, and hard to find (if you wrote them down). Don't use the Stored Passwords feature of AOL, as that removes one of the two locks on your Quick Checkout access, and don't use the same password for your AOL account and Quick Checkout.

Shopping with Credit Cards and the Alternatives

To shop online, you need a credit card (or a bank/debit card with the Visa or MasterCard symbol on it). All the stores that we surveyed take credit cards, specifically Visa, MasterCard, and American Express. Some stores accept Discover, including all Quick Checkout stores. Some stores, such as barnesandnoble.com, also accept Diners Club, JCB, and corporate purchasing cards.

Some (but not many) AOL stores accept checks and money orders, and some of the stores also issue and/or accept gift certificates.

Shopping the Classifieds and AOL Direct

Is your attic overflowing with really great stuff, or do you need some really great stuff so you can fill your attic? Either way, AOL's ClassifiedPlus is a great place to start (and finish). Over 55 million AOL and Internet users have access to the ClassifiedPlus listings. You can access ClassifiedPlus by using the Keyword: **Classifieds**.

The ClassifiedPlus main page, shown in Figure 8-4, is clean and easy to use. Here are some of your options:

- Place an ad (and change or delete one if you wish).
- Subscribe to the ClassifiedPlus newsletter.
- Access extensive customer service information.
- Jump into any of the ten main classifieds categories.

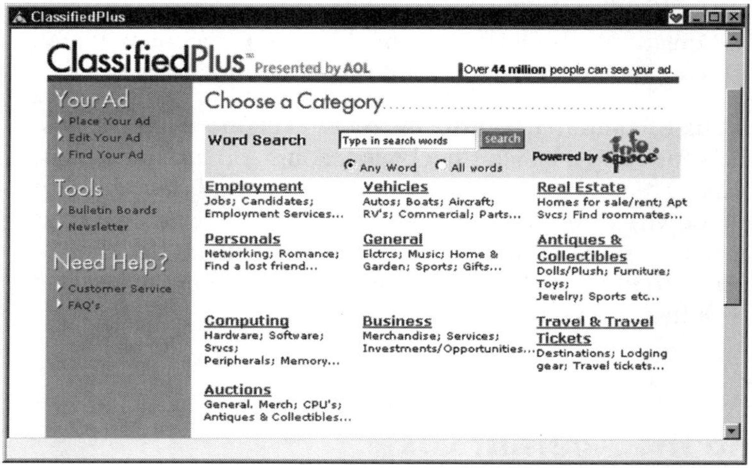

Figure 8-4. Choose a category or place an ad on the ClassifiedPlus main page.

At the specially-discounted AOL member rates (you must be using your AOL account and its built-in browser to qualify for the rates), you pay from around $2 to $25 for a two-week listing, depending on what you're advertising.

Chapter 9

Discovering AOL Channels

In This Chapter

- Surfing the AOL Channels
- Touring the "serious" channels
- Site-seeing in the "fun" channels

AOL is overflowing with information on an incredible array of topics, from business and finance to health and hobbies. Whether you're looking for formal lessons, browsing around on your own, or hankering to join a community dedicated to your favorite pastime, AOL has something for you in one of its 18 channels.

An Introduction to Using Channels

AOL channels are similar to those you find on your television, but with two important differences. First, AOL channels are huge, containing vast amounts of information. Second, AOL channels are interactive — all contain message boards, chat rooms, and ways to get involved.

Flipping the channels at AOL is nearly as simple as changing channels on your television. Each main channel window comes equipped with a remote control — an identical set of buttons arrayed down the left side of the window (see Figure 9-1).

Click any channel button to reach that channel.

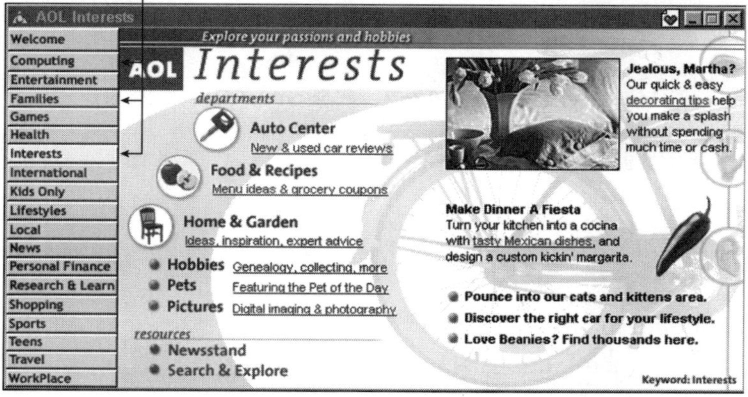

Figure 9-1: All main channel windows offer you buttons to reach the other channels.

Click once, and the screen is instantly converted to the desired channel. If you don't flip for that method, AOL offers several more:

- Click the Channels icon on the AOL toolbar and then choose the desired channel from the menu.
- Type the channel name into the text box on the navigation bar and click Go (or press Enter).
- Use Keyword: **Channels**. The Channels window has a large, colorful button for every channel.

Welcome

The AOL Welcome screen is the perfect jumping-off spot for your daily online travels. It's fully integrated into the button bar that you find at the left of the main screen of every channel (and on the Welcome screen itself).

The Welcome screen greets you with buttons and links to top news stories, important search and help resources, and the enticing Today on AOL section, featuring all sorts of juicy information, contests, and merchandise.

Computing

AOL's Computing Channel (Keyword: **Computing**) is founded on a very basic truth: If you're using AOL, you're using a computer, and the more you know about your computer, the more you'll get out of your AOL experience. The Computing Channel's help desk (Keyword: **Get Help Now**) and online classrooms have a lot to offer.

Tip: A recent addition to AOL Computing is CNET (Keyword: **CNET**), known for its computer-oriented television programming and extensive Web sites dedicated to (you'll never guess in a million years, will you?) . . . computers!

Entertainment

The Entertainment Channel (Keyword: **Entertainment** or **ENT**) really speaks (and sings, and dances, and performs) for itself. TV listings, music sites, show times, movie reviews, concert dates, or celebrity news — you name it, the Entertainment Channel has it. If your town (like ours) has only a few good theaters and you have to phone each one to listen to their barely audible recorded listings, you're going to love using MovieFone to find out what's on at the movies:

1. Get to MovieFone by using Keyword: **MovieFone**.
2. Type your zip code.
3. Choose any other search criteria from either drop-down list box.
4. Click Go.

Families

If family ties are tying you down, the Families Channel (Keyword: **Family**) may have the solution. The channel provides resources, support, and access to experts on the topic of family, all from the comfort of your family nest. Parent Soup (Keyword: **PS**) is a heart-warming forum for parents, whether they are parents-to-be or parents of teens. Resources include news, articles, tips, databases, newsletters, message boards, and chats. The Genealogy Forum (Keyword: **Roots**) is an incredible resource of helpful guides, surname and family history files and databases, and a community of fellow genealogists.

Games

The Games Channel (Keyword: **Games**) is total fun and games, 24 hours a day, 7 days a week, 365 days a year. Try out the Games Parlor (Keyword: **Parlor**), which offers classic parlor games you can play online (for an additional hourly charge):

Backgammon

Bridge

Cribbage

Hearts

Poker

If you prefer action and adventure games, make Xtreme Games your Holy Grail (Keyword: **Xtreme**). Like the Game Parlor, Xtreme Games charge an hourly fee but are a bit more expensive. You can find such games as

- Air Warrior III (aerial shoot 'em up game)
- Dragon's Gate (text-based adventure game)
- Warcraft II (graphic-based strategy game)

If you love games, but don't have the money for the premium games, head for Game Shows Online (Keyword: **Game Shows**), where you find a collection of no-charge games such as NTN Studio (trivia), Puzzle Zone (word puzzles), and Slingo (a cross between bingo and a word game).

Health

The virtual road to wellness begins at the Health Channel (Keyword: **Health**). The channel offers healthy coverage of conditions and their treatments, and experts and support groups, as well as nutrition, fitness, health care, and alternative medicine. Thrive Online (Keyword: **Thrive**) is a hip, straight-to-the-point wellness forum offering resources on physical, emotional, and sexual health.

Interests

If nothing in this chapter has tickled your fancy yet, odds are you'll find something to fancy in the Interests Channel (Keyword: **Interests**). This is the catch-all channel, covering virtually every hobby that doesn't already have a channel.

- The Pets forum (Keyword: **Pets,** see Figure 9-2) is an invaluable resource for pet lovers. Get assistance choosing, naming, caring for, and training your pet.

Figure 9-2. Check out the Pet of the Day at AOL Pets.

- The Food forum (Keyword: **Food**) offers thousands of recipes, guides to healthy living, and information on local dining. You can even share your own recipes.
- Home & Garden forum (Keyword: **Home**) offers tips, advice, and information on gardening, home improvement, and decorating.

International

The folks at AOL International have knit together in-depth guides to interesting places all over the world, combining travel, economic, cultural, and political information in an easy-to-use format. Thanks to AOL's International Channel (Keyword: **Intl**), the entire world is only seconds away.

Kids Only

As the sign says, Kids Only (Keyword: **Kids**) is a channel for kids only. Technically, parents and adults can sneak in while the kids aren't looking, but the entire channel is really geared for the young ones and offers these feature areas:

News&Sports	Art Studio
Clubs	TV, Movies, & Music
Games	Homework Help

Note: Adults can enter Kids Only and participate and interact with the kids; however, Kids Only is intended for kids. The staff and community leaders work hard to make this a safe and comfortable place for kids, but parents also need to monitor their children's activities online.

Lifestyles

The Lifestyles Channel is all about identity. If you know yourself, you'll also know exactly where you want to be in the Lifestyles Channel. The channel offers departments dedicated to virtually every lifestyle, including those focused on gender, age, religion, ethnicity, and sexual orientation. For example, Ages & Stages (Keyword: **Ages**) covers virtually every age and generation, from Generation X to the "Third Age."

Local

AOL offers local city guides (Keyword: **Local**), delivering everything from local news, traffic, movie listings, and dining-out guides to personal ads, job listings, and a real estate section. Many local guides are produced in cooperation with local newspapers, magazines, or TV stations — organizations that know their towns very well. Go directly to the local guide for your city by using the city's name as a keyword or by choosing your city from the list box.

News

AOL News is your route to what's happening now throughout the world (Keyword: **News**). The channel gathers news from many of the top sources online, in print, and on the air. Among AOL's news gathering partners are CBS News, National Public Radio, TIME magazine, The New York Times, the Associated Press, Reuters, and Bloomberg. The AOL News Channel screen is packed tightly with news headlines and features, and the News Search feature can find hundreds of articles on a given topic.

Personal Finance

AOL Personal Finance (Keyword: **PF**) is for the homeowner, the stockholder, and the just-plain-everyday person striving to make the most of his or her economic resources. AOL packs just about everything an investor needs to track the stock market, individual stocks, and a personal portfolio in one small, unassuming box at Keyword: **Quotes**. Every screen name on an AOL account can maintain up to 20 online portfolios that are easy to track at Keyword: **My Portfolios**. And the Market News Center (Keyword: **MNC**) is a one-stop shop for current events in the major financial markets.

Research & Learn

Whether you need general reference resources or help with schoolwork, college admissions, enhancing your child's education, or furthering your own professional education, AOL's Research & Learn is a great place to turn. This channel (Keyword: **Research**) is home base to the Merriam-Webster Collegiate Dictionary online (Keyword: **Dictionary**) and offers a handy collection of encyclopedias and other desktop references.

Sports

If you're into sports, as a spectator or participant, you'll want to get into the Sports Channel (Keyword: **Sports**). The Scoreboard (Keyword: **Scoreboard**) offers virtually every major and minor league game score — all up-to-date and accurate. If you love to talk sports, we have to talk . . . about the Grandstand (Keyword: **GS**). This forum's main events are the message board and chat rooms, in which discussions between sports fans take the field. The Grandstand even hosts fantasy leagues to put you in the middle of the action.

Teens

Teenagers have their own hangout at the Teens Channel (Keyword: **Teens**), a collection of news, entertainment, chat rooms, fashion, and friends. Features include Teen People (an online version of the magazine), AOgirl ("an AOL just for the girls"), and links to teen-related areas throughout AOL.

Travel

The Travel Channel (Keyword: **Travel**) is a destination designed for travelers, whether their trips are for pleasure or business. In this channel, you find everything you need to plan the perfect trip, from information on vacation resorts and exotic ports to traveler reports and news of all sorts.

Tip

Once you've decided where you want to go, make your reservations at Travelocity in the Travel Channel. This online travel agency lets you search and book flights, rental cars, hotel rooms, and packages — right from your computer.

WorkPlace

On the WorkPlace Channel (Keyword: **WorkPlace**), you may find energetic entrepreneurs founding small businesses and career-minded workers striving to succeed in big business. You can turn to the WorkPlace Channel's Start-Up Businesses department (Keyword: **StartUp**) for an array of resources that will keep you one step ahead of the pack. Or if your career is already firmly established, the WorkPlace Channel stands ready to help you update your skills, network with your peers, and enjoy a daily dose of Dilbert.

Appendix A: AOL Keywords

Keywords are shortcuts to thousands of destinations — fast and easy. Type the keyword in the text box on the navigation bar at the top of your screen, click Go (or press Enter), and off you go!

Cross-Reference: If you're not yet familiar with keywords, refer to Chapter 2.

The only problem with keywords is that you need to know them *before* you can use them. AOL maintains lists of keywords online at Keyword: **Keyword**. To save you some trouble, we compiled a list of popular and useful keywords here. Do keep in mind that keywords come and go over time. If you encounter a keyword that no longer works, go to Keyword: **Keyword** to check for a new one.

:-)
The Friendly Face

;)
Hecklers Online

?
QuickStart: A Guide for New Members

<><
Christianity Online

9
AOL Long Distance

911
Public Safety Center

A&R
Addiction & Recovery Forum

A&V
Animation & Video Forums

ABL
AOL Pro Basketball

ABOUT CHAT
Chatting Online

ABOUT SO
About Special Olympics

ABUSE OF WOMEN
Domestic Abuse: Helping Men Heal

ACCESS
Access Numbers

ACTIVISM
Volunteerism

ACUPUNCTURE
Acupuncture

ADD
Attention Deficit Disorder

ADDICT
Addictions

ADDRESS BOOK
Address Book

ADVANCED COMPUTERS
Advanced Computers & Technology

ADVENTURE TRAVEL
Adventure and Outdoor Travel Forum

ADVICE
Advice & Tips

AEROBICS
AOL Fitness

AGES
Ages & Stages

AGNOSTIC
AOL Religion:Atheism

AHH
Alternatives: Health and Healing

AHL
AOL Hockey

AIDS
AIDS & HIV

AIDSLINE
AIDS Line

AIM
AOL Instant Messenger

AIM PASS
Change Your AOL Instant Messenger Password

AIR TRAVEL
Airlines Center

AIRFARE
Air Fares

ALA
American Lung Assocation

ALCOHOL
Alcoholism

ALL HEALTH
All Health

ALL APARTMENTS
Apartment Locators

ALLERGIES
Allergy & Respiratory Disorders

ALTERNATIVE MEDICINE
Alternative Medicine Forum

ALUMNI
Alumni

ALZHEIMERS
Alzheimer's Disease

AMERICAN DIABETES
American Diabetes

AMERICAS PARKS
America's Parks

ANCESTOR
Genealogy

ANEMIA
Anemia

ANIMAL
Pets Forum

ANOREXIA
Eating Disorders

ANSWER
AOL Member Services

ANTIQUE
Collectors Corner Exchange

ANXIETY
Anxiety & Panic Disorders

AOGIRL
AOL Teens:AOgirl

AOL 2.7
AOL 2.7

AOL 3.0
AOL 3.0

AOL ANNUAL PLAN
AOL Annual Pricing Plans

AOL AUSTRIA
AOL Austria

AOL AUTO CENTER
AOL Auto Center

AOL BASICS
Learn How To Use AOL And Your Computer

AOL BEGINNERS
Tutorial

AOL BUSINESS DIRECTORY
AOL Business Directory

AOL CHAT
People Connection

AOL CLASSIFIED
Classifieds

AOL CREDIT ALERT
AOL Credit Alert Area

AOL CREDIT CARD
AOL Card

AOL DIAG
AOL Diagnostic Tool

AOL FAMILIES
Families Channel

AOL FOUNDATION
AOL Foundation

AOL GAMES
Games Channel

AOL GAMES STORE
AOL Games Store/AOL Store

AOL GERMANY
AOL Germany

AOL GIRL
AOL Teens: Girls

AOL GLOSSARY
AOL Glossary

AOL HOMETOWN
Hometown AOL

AOL HOT GAMES
AOL Hot Games Collection

AOL INSIDER
AOL Insider Tips

AOL JOBS
Finding A Job

AOL LD BILLING
AOL Long Distance Billing

AOL LIVE
Today In AOL Live

AOL LIVE QUICK START
AOL Live Quick Start

AOL LONG DISTANCE BILLING
AOL Long Distance Members Area

AOL MARKET TALK
AOL Market Talk

AOL MARKETDAY
AOL Marketday

AOL NEIGHBORHOOD WATCH
AOL Neighborhood Watch

AOL NETMARKET
AOL Netmarket

AOL PERSONALS
The Romance Channel, Your Area For Love!

AOL SA
Shoppers Advantage

AOL SAVINGS CLUB
AOL Savings Clubs

AOL SCUBA
AOL Scuba Forum

AOL SECRETS
AOL Secrets

AOL SHOP DIRECTS UPGRADE SHOP
Upgrade Store / AOL Shop Direct

AOL SHOPPERS ADVANTAGE
Shoppers Advantage

AOL SHOPPING
AOL Shopping Channel

AOL STORE
AOL Store

AOL SUPER STORE
Shoppers Advantage

AOL SWITZERLAND
AOL Switzerland

AOL TEENS
AOL Teens Channel

AOL TODAY
AOL Today

AOL UPDATE
AOL System Update

AOL VISA
AOL Visa Card

AOL W
AOL Headquarters Weather

AOL WEBOPAEDIA
Webopaedia

AOLS INSTAKISS
Instakiss - Love@AOL Virtual Kiss

APARTMENT
Real Estate Center, Renting Area

ARCHAEOLOGY
Archaeology Forum

ARCHIVE PHOTOS
Archive Photos

AROMATHERAPY
Aromatherapy

ART
Arts and Leisure

ART STUDIO
Kids Only Art Studio

ASTHMA
Asthma

ASTROLOGY
Astrology & Divination

ASTRONOMY
Astronomy Club

ATLAS
Geography & Maps

ATTORNEY
Legal Professionals

AUCTION
Auctions & Outlets

AUDIO BOOK CLUB
Audio Book Club

AUTHOR@AOL
Ongoing Author Series with Barnes & Noble

AUTHORING TOOLS
Home Page Publishing Tools

AUTISM
Autism

AUTO BUYING
Auto Center Buying Guide

AUTO CLASSIFIED
AOL Classifieds Automobiles

AUTO SHOP
Shopping Channel Auto Shop

AUTOCAD
Cad Resource Center

AV
AOL AutoVantage

AVIATION
Aviation & Aeronautics

B&C
Books and Culture

BABIES
Babies

BASEBALL
AOL Baseball

BASICS
Learn How To Use AOL

BEGINNER
Help Desk Area

BEST OF AOL
Best Of AOL

BETA APPLY
Apply to be a Beta Tester

BEYOND
Beyond.com on AOL

BICYCLES
Bicycling

BILLING
Billing

BLOCK JUNK MAIL
Junk Mail

BN
Barnes & Noble Booksellers

BOOK
Books Community

BOOKCENTRAL
Book and Author Information And Discussion

BOOKSTORE
Bookstore

BUDDY LIST
Buddy List

BUDDY VIEW
View your Buddy List

BUILD YOUR WEB PAGE
Building Home Pages

BUSINESS NEWS
Business News Center

BUSINESS TRAVELER
Business Travel Center

CALL AOL
AOL Telephone Support

CAMPING
Parks and Camping

CANCEL
Account Cancellation Requests

CANDIDATE
Election 2000

CARDS
Cards

CAREER
Your Career

CARPAL TUNNEL
Carpal Tunnel Syndrome

CATARACTS
Cataracts

CATHOLIC
Catholic Community

CB
College Board

CHANNEL GUIDE
Channel Guide

CHILDCARE
Family Living

CHILDRENS TV
Family Entertainment

CHILD-SUPPORT
Families Going Through A Separation or Divorce

CHRISTIAN
Christianity Spirituality Department

CHRONIC PAIN
Chronic Pain

CLASSES
Online Classroom Class Schedule

CLOSEDFUNDS
Closed-End Funds

COLLECTING
Hobby Central: Collecting

COLLEGES
College Prep Area

COMMON COLD
Common Cold

COMMUNITIES
Lifestyles Communitites

COMPUTER CLASS
Computing - Online Classroom

COMPUTER TIPS
Computing Tips

COMPUTING
AOL Computing Channel

CONCERTS
Concerts & Tours

CONTEST
Contests

COUNTRIES
Countries

COURSES
Courses Online

CROSS-COUNTRY
Cross Country Travel Tips

CULTURE FINDER
Culture Finder

CURRENCY CONVERTER
Currency Converter

DEAF COMMUNITY
Deaf Community

DEPRESSION
Depression

DESKTOP PUBLISHING
Desktop & Web Publishing Forums

DESTINATIONS
AOL Travel: Destinations

DIABETES
Diabetes

DIET
Dieting & Weight Loss

DINNER
What's For Dinner

DISABILITIES
Conditions & Treatments

DOCTORS
Doctors And Insurance

DYSLEXIA
Dyslexia

ENCYCLOPEDIA
Encyclopedia

ENTERTAINMENT
Entertainment Channel

FAMILY
AOL Families Channel

FARE WARS
Fare Wars

FAST FACTS
AOL Fast Facts

FAVORITE PLACES
Favorite Places

FIBROMYALGIA
Fibromyalgia

FILE SEARCH
Download Center

FINANCIAL AID
Education Financial Aid

FIND A JOB
Find a Job

FIRST TIME SHOPPER
First Time Shopper

FISHING
Fishing

FLU
Influenza

FOOD
AOL Food

FOOTBALL
AOL Pro Football

FOREIGN DICTIONARY
Foreign Dictionary

FRIEND
Sign On A Friend

FTP
File Transfer Protocol (ftp)

FUND
Mutual Fund Center

GALLERY
AOL Hometown:The Gallery Community Center

GAME SHOWS
Games Channel: Game Shows

GAMES
AOL Games Channel

GAMING
Online Gaming Forums

GAY
Gay & Lesbian

GET HELP NOW
AOL Computing: Get Help Now

GIFT REMINDER
Reminder Service

GIFTS
Gifts And Gadgets

GLENNA
Glennas Garden: Cancer Support Forum

GLOBALNET
International Access

GLOSSARY
Glossary

GOLF
AOL Golf

GOVERNMENT
Law & Government

GPF HELP
Member Services Error Messages

GRAD SCHOOL
Graduate School

GRANDSTAND
AOL Grandstand

GRAPHICS
Computing Graphic Arts Forum

GREETING CARDS
Flowers & Cards

GS SOCCER
AOL Grandstand: Soccer

GUARANTEE
AOL Shopping Guarantee

HAIR LOSS
Baldness & Hair Loss

HEALTH
Health Channel

HEALTH INSURANCE
Health Insurance

HEALTHY EATING
Healthy Eating

HEART
Heart & Blood Disorders

HELP CLASS
AOL Help Class

HIGH SCHOOL
College Bound: Seniors Only

HIGH SPEED
High Speed Access

HOBBY
Hobby Central

HOLIDAYS
Holidays @ AOL

HOROSCOPES
Horoscopes

HOW TO DOWNLOAD
How to Download

HURRICANE
AOL Weather: Hurricanes

HYPERTENSION
Hypertension/High Blood Pressure

I NEED HELP
Notify AOL

IA
Insomniacs Asylum

INFO CENTER
Download Info Center

INTERESTS
AOL Interests Channel

INTERNATIONAL GRANDSTAND
AOL International: Grandstand

INTERNET
Internet Connection

INTL
AOL International Channel

INTL NEWS
International News

INTL TRAVEL
International Travel

INVESTING BASICS
Investing Basics

JAZZ
Jazz

JEWISH
Jewish Community Online

KEYWORD
Keyword List

KIDS
Kids Only Channel

LAST MINUTE GIFTS
Quick Gifts Screen

LAW RESOURCES
Legal Resources

LEADERS
AOL Community Leaders

LEARN AUTO AOL
Learn Automatic AOL

LEARN CHAT
Learn People Connection

LEARN DOWNLOAD
Learn Downloading

LEARN EMAIL
Learn E-mail

LEARN GETTING AROUND
Learn Getting Around

LEARN KEYWORD
Learn Keywords

LEARN PARENT
Learn Parental Controls

LEARN QUOTES
Learn Quotes

LESBIAN
Gay & Lesbian

LIFESTYLES
AOL Lifestyles Channel

LIVE
Today In AOL Live

LOAN CENTER
Loan Center

LOCAL
AOL Local Channel

LOTTERY
Lottery

LOVE
Love@AOL

MAIL CENTER
Post Office

MAIL CONTROLS
Mail Controls

MAIL EXTRAS
Mail Extras

MANIC
Bipolar Disorder/Manic Depression

MARKET NEWS CENTER
Market News Center

MEDIA CENTER
Media Center

MEDICAL DICTIONARY
Medical Dictionary

MEMBER OPINIONS
AOL Travel: Member Opinions

MEMBER PERKS
AOL Member Perks

MEMBERS
AOL Member Directory

MO
Moms Online

MOVIE SHOWTIMES
Local Movie Info

MOVIES
Movies

MUSIC
AOL Music

MY BOARDS
Manage Your Message Boards

MY CALENDAR
My Calendar

MY FTP SPACE
FTP Space

MY HOMEPAGE
Personal Publisher

MY PORTFOLIOS
Portfolios

NAMES
Screen Names

NEW
What's New on AOL

NEW MOVIE
New Movie Releases

NEWS
AOL News Channel

NEWS SEARCH
Search the News

NEWSGROUPS
Internet Newsgroups

NEWSLETTERS
Newsletters

NEWSSTAND
The Newsstand

ONLINE CAMPUS
Online Campus

ONLINE CLASSROOMS
AOL Computing: Online Classroom

ONLINE INVESTOR
Online Investor

ONLY ON AOL
Only On AOL

OPERATING SYSTEMS
The Operating Systems Area

PARENTAL CONTROLS
Parental Controls

PARENTING
Families Main Screen

PARKS
Americas Parks

PARTY PLANNING
AOL Classifieds Party Planning Center

PASSWORD
Change Your Password

PC HELP
Computing PC Help Area

PERSONAL FINANCE
Personal Finance Channel

PETS
Pets

PF
AOL Personal Finance

PICTURES
You've Got Pictures

PORTFOLIOS
Stock Portfolio

POST OFFICE
AOL Mail Center

POSTCARD
Online Greetings

POSTMASTER
AOL Postmaster

POWERTOOLS
Powertools For AOL

PREFERENCES
My AOL

PREFERRED MAIL
Preferred Mail

PRICING PLANS
New Pricing Plans

PRINTER
Printer Resource Center

PRIVACY
AOL Privacy Policy

PROFILE
Change Profile

QUARTERLY REVIEW
Mutual Fund Quarterly Review

QUICK CHECKOUT
AOL Quick Checkout

QUICKSTART
AOL New Members Quick Start

RACING
Auto Racing

RAILROADING
Model Planes/trains

REFUND
AOL Access Refund Policy

RELIGION
Religion & Beliefs Channel

RENTALS
AOL Rental Classifieds

RESEARCH
Research and Learn Channel

RESERVATIONS
AOL Travel Reservation Center

RESUME
Post A Resume Feature Package

REWARDS
AOL Rewards

ROADMAPS
Maps And Directions

SBA
US Small Business Administration

SCOREBOARD
AOL Sports Scoreboards

SCOUTS
Scouting

SEARCH
AOL Search

SHOP DIRECT
AOL Shop Direct

SOFTWARE
Download Software

SONGS
Music

SOUND
PC Music & Sound Forum

SPAM
E-mail Spam Information

SPIRITUALITY
Spirituality

SPORTS
AOL Sports Channel

SPORTS INVESTOR
What Smart Sports Fans Do On AOL

SPORTS NEWS
Sports News Front Page

STAMPS
Stamp Collecting

STARTING YOUR BUSINESS
Getting Started

STOCKS
Quotes & Portfolio

STREP THROAT
Strep Throat

STRESS
Emotional Well-being

SUGGESTIONS
Suggestion Boxes

SUPPORT
Member Services

SUPPORT GROUPS
Health Support Groups

SYSTEM RESPONSE
System Response Report

TAXES
Tax Planning

TEENS
Teens Channel

THEME PARKS
Theme Parks

TIME FOR KIDS
Time For Kids

TODAYS NEWS
Today's News

TODDLER
Parenting Toddlers

TOS
Terms Of Service

TRAVEL
Travel Channel

TRAVEL DESTINATIONS
Where To Go, What To Do

TRAVEL WARNINGS
Travel Advisories

TUBERCULOSIS
Tuberculosis

TV SHOWS
TV Shows

UPGRADE
The Latest AOL Software

USER GROUPS
User Groups Forum

VACATIONS
Travel

VEGETARIAN
Vegetarians Online

VIEWERS
Recommended Viewers

VIRUS
Virus Information

VIRUS INFO
AOL Virus Info Area

WEB
World Wide Web

WEB BUSINESS
Doing Business Online

WEB HELP
Member Services: Net Help

WEB PUBLISHING
Building Home Pages

WEB TUTORIAL
Web Tutorials

WEDDING
Weddings

WELCOME
Welcome Screen

WHATS NEW
What's Hot and What's New On AOL

WHITE PAGES
White Pages

WINE & DINE ONLINE
Food and Drink Network

WOMEN
AOL Women

WORKING WEB
Your Business: Working The Web

WRITER
The Writers Club

WRITERS CLUB MARKETPLACE
Writers Club Marketplace

YACHTING
Boating

YP
Yellow Pages

ZIP CODE
Zip Code Directory

ZOO
Zoos and Aquariums

Glossary

A

access number
A phone number (usually local) that your modem uses to access America Online. To find an access number online, go to Keyword: **Access**. If you aren't able to sign on to America Online, see Appendix A.

address
An e-mail address that allows you to send an e-mail to anyone on America Online or anywhere on the Internet. You can look up addresses for America Online members at Keyword: **Members**, and addresses for Internet denizens at various places on the World Wide Web. See also *URL*.

Address Book
An AOL software feature that allows you to store e-mail addresses for easy access. Your Address Book may be created, edited, or used through the Address Book icon available when composing mail.

attached file
A file that hitches a ride with a sent or forwarded e-mail message. Whether the file is text, sound, or pictures, it is said to be attached if it has been included with the e-mail for separate downloading by the recipient.

Automatic AOL (Auto AOL)
An automated feature that can send and receive your e-mail and files, as well as receive newsgroup postings. Auto AOL can be set up to run anytime, including while you are online. It is accessible under your Mail menu.

B

blind courtesy copy (bcc)
A feature of the America Online e-mail system that allows you to send e-mail to a member or members without the primary addressee's knowledge.

browser
A component of your AOL software that allows you to access the World Wide Web.

Buddy List
A special list that stores your "buddies" (screen names of friends, family members, coworkers, and so on) and informs you when they sign on or off America Online.

C

cache
A portion of a data storage device, RAM, or processor set aside to temporarily hold recently or frequently accessed information — usually done to improve system performance.

channel
This is the broadest category of information into which America Online organizes its content. See Keyword: **Channels** for an interactive list or Keyword: **Channel Guide** for listings of the areas within each channel.

chat
To engage in real-time communications with other members. America Online members that are online at the same time may chat in a number of ways, including Instant Messages (IMs) and chat/conference rooms.

chat room
An online area where members may meet to communicate and interact with others. There are two kinds of chat rooms: public and private. You find public chat rooms in the People Connection area (Keyword: **People**) or in the many forums around America Online (see Keyword: **AOL Live**).

courtesy copy (cc)
A feature of the America Online e-mail system that allows you to address e-mail to a member for whom the e-mail is not directly intended or is of secondary interest. The primary addressee(s) are aware that the copy was made, similar to the carbon copy in business correspondence.

Customer Relations
The number for America Online's Customer Relations Hotline is 800-827-6364. The billing and technical assistance departments are open 24 hours a day. The Terms of Service, Community Action Team, and screen name departments are open 9 a.m. to 12 a.m. Eastern time, 7 days a week.

D

Delete
An America Online e-mail system feature that allows you to permanently remove a piece of mail from any and all of your mailboxes. The Delete feature is useful for removing unneeded mail from your Old Mail box.

domain
Used in Internet addresses and analogous to a city in a postal address. In e-mail addresses, usually everything to the right of the @ symbol is referred to as the domain. For example, the domain for America Online member addresses is `aol.com`. See also address, e-mail, e-mail address, and Internet.

download
The transfer of information stored on a remote computer to a storage device on your personal computer. This information can come from America Online via its file libraries, or from other America Online members via attached files in e-mail.

Download Manager
An AOL software feature that allows you to keep a queue of files to download at a later time. You can even set up your software to download at specific times and automatically sign off when downloading is complete.

E

e-mail
Short for electronic mail. One of the most popular features of online services, e-mail allows you to send private communications electronically from one person to another. See Keyword: **Mail Center**.

e-mail address
A cyberspace mailbox. On America Online, your e-mail address is simply your screen name; for folks outside America Online, your address is your screen name with `@aol.com` after it.

F

favorite place
A feature that allows you to "mark" America Online and World Wide Web sites you'd like to return to later. Store these in your Favorite Places list and include any Web site or any America Online window with a red heart in the upper-right corner.

forum
A place online where members with similar interests may find valuable information, exchange ideas, share files, and get help on a particular area of interest.

FTP
Acronym for File Transfer Protocol. A method of transferring files to and from a computer that is connected to the Internet. America Online offers FTP access via the Keyword: **FTP**, as well as personal FTP sites at Keyword: **My Place**.

H

home page
1. The first "page" in a Web site. 2. Your own page on the Web. Every member on America Online can now create his or her own home page — see Keyword: **My Home Page**. 3. The page you go to when you first enter the Web.

html
Acronym for HyperText Markup Language. This is the language used in creating most Web pages and is interpreted by the AOL Web browser to display those pages.

http
Acronym for HyperText Transport Protocol.

I

Ignore
1. A way of blocking a member's chat from your view in a chat/conference room window. Ignore is most useful when the chat of another member becomes disruptive in the chat room. Note that the Ignore button does not block or ignore IMs from a member — it only blocks the text from your own view in a chat or conference room.
2. An AOL software e-mail system feature that allows you to ignore mail in your New Mail box, causing it to be moved to your Old Mail box without reading it first.

IM (Instant Message)
America Online's equivalent of passing notes during a meeting, as opposed to speaking up in the room (chat) or writing out a memo (e-mail). Internet users can send and receive Instant Messages if they download and install the free AOL Instant Messenger program (Keyword: **AIM**).

Internet
The mother of all networks is not an online service itself, but serves to interconnect worldwide computer systems and networks. The Internet, originally operated by the National Science Foundation (NSF), is now managed by private companies (like America Online). To obtain more information about the Internet, use the Keyword: **Internet**.

ISP
Acronym for Internet service provider. An ISP generally provides a point to which you can connect and access various Internet-based services such as Web sites, FTP, e-mail, gopher, and newsgroups. See also FTP, newsgroup, and World Wide Web.

K

Keep As New
An America Online e-mail system feature that allows you to keep mail in your New Mail box, even after you've read or ignored it.

keyboard shortcuts
The AOL software provides keyboard command equivalents for menu choices. For example, instead of choosing Instant Message from the People Menu on the toolbar, press Ctrl+I on Windows or ⌘+I on the Mac.

keyword
A fast way to move around within America Online. For example, you can go directly to the Games channel by using the Keyword: **Games**. To use a keyword, type it into the text box in the navigation bar and click Go. Or press ⌘+K on the Mac or Ctrl+K on the PC, type the keyword, and press the Return or Enter key.

L

library
An area online in which files may be uploaded to and downloaded from. The files may be of any type: text, graphics, software, sounds, and so on. These files can be downloaded from America Online's host computer to your personal computer's hard disk or floppy disk. To search libraries available for your platform, go to Keyword: **Download Center** and click Shareware.

link
A pointer to another place that takes you there when you activate it (usually by clicking it). America Online has literally thousands of links that crisscross the service, but they can't compare to the millions of links on the Web (often called hyperlinks) that can cross continents.

M

mail controls
A set of preferences that enable the master account holder to control mail receipt for any screen name on the account. To access controls, go to Keyword: **Mail Controls.** You can block junk mail from your e-mailbox at Keyword: **Preferred Mail**.

Member Directory
The database of America Online member screen names that have profiles. To be included in this database, a member need only create a Member

Profile. The Member Directory is located at Keyword: **Members**.

message board
An area where members can post messages to exchange information, ask a question, or reply to another message. Message boards are organized by messages (in sequential order) that relate to specific subjects within topics.

N

newsgroup
Internet's version of a public message board. Available on America Online at Keyword: **Newsgroups**.

P

Parental Controls
Keyword: **Parental Control** enables the master account holder to restrict access to certain areas and features on America Online (such as blocking Instant Messages and chat rooms) for any screen name on the account. Once Parental Controls are set for a particular screen name, they are active each time that screen name signs on.

password
The secret 6-to-8-character code word that you use to secure your account. Never reveal your password to anyone, even those claiming to be AOL employees.

Personal Filing Cabinet (PFC)
A special feature of the AOL software that organizes your e-mail, as well as message board and newsgroup postings. Everything in your Personal Filing Cabinet is stored on your hard drive; set PFC preferences by clicking the My AOL icon and choosing Personal Filing Cabinet.

S

screen name
Names that identify America Online members online. Screen names are set up under a master screen name (Keyword: **Names**), may contain between 3 and 16 characters, and must be unique. Any account may have up to seven screen names, and each can (and should) have its own unique password.

T

toolbar
The row of buttons in the AOL software, usually found at the top of your screen. In AOL software versions 4.0 and 5.0, many of the buttons have menus and portions of the toolbar are customizable.

TOS
Short for America Online's Terms of Service — the rules everyone agrees to when registering and setting up any member account on America Online. You can read these terms at Keyword: **TOS**.

U

URL
An address for an online resource, such as a Web site or an America Online page. URL stands for Uniform Resource Locator. You can enter a URL address directly into the text box on the navigation bar or in the keyword window.

V

virus
Computer software that has the capability to attach itself to other software or files, does so without the permission or knowledge of the user, and is generally designed with one intent — to propagate itself. Virus prevention software and information can be found at Keyword: **Virus**.

W

World Wide Web (WWW)
An overarching term for the many Internet files that are displayed and linked together via a special protocol called HyperText Transfer Protocol (or HTTP). World Wide Web information is available on America Online, by using URL addresses to get to various Web sites or pages.

INDEX

E

F

G

H

I